Nuclear and
Particle Physics

Bryan Milner

Series editor: David Sang

CAMBRIDGE
UNIVERSITY PRESS

PUBLISHED BY THE PRESS SYNDICATE OF THE UNIVERSITY OF CAMBRIDGE
The Pitt Building, Trumpington Street, Cambridge, United Kingdom

CAMBRIDGE UNIVERSITY PRESS
The Edinburgh Building, Cambridge CB2 2RU, UK
40 West 20th Street, New York, NY 10011-4211, USA
10 Stamford Road, Oakleigh, VIC 3166, Australia
Ruiz de Alarcón 13, 28014 Madrid, Spain
Dock House, The Waterfront, Cape Town 8001,
South Africa

http://www.cambridge.org

First published 2001

Printed in the United Kingdom
at the University Press, Cambridge

Typeface Swift   *System* QuarkXPress®

A catalogue record for this book is
available from the British Library

ISBN 0 521 79837 X paperback

Designed and produced by Gecko Ltd, Bicester, Oxon

Front cover photograph: Technician working on
OPAL detector at CERN, Science Photo Library

Acknowledgements

17*l*, 17*r*, 41*r*, 43, Hulton Getty; 41*l*, Mary Evans Picture
Library; 49, TRH Pictures; 50*bl*, Science Museum/
Science & Society Pic Lib; 50*tr*, 59*tr*, 60*tr*, Laurent
Guiraud/CERN; 55*t*, Stanford Linear Accelerator
Center/Science Photo Library; 55*b*, Peter Menzel/Science
Photo Library; 56*t*, Lawrence Berkeley Laboratory/
Science Photo Library; 56*b*, by kind permission of
Kernfysisch Versneller Instituut, Netherlands; 59*bl*,
Fermilab/Science Photo Library; 60*br*, Adam Hart-
Davis/Science Photo Library; 67, Klaus Guldbrandsen/
Science Photo Library

Contents

Acknowledgements ii

Introduction iv

1 The structure of the nucleus 1
Nuclear structure and nuclear reactions:
a review of basic ideas 1
What force holds atomic nuclei together? 5
The radii of atomic nuclei 6
The density of nuclear matter 7
Looking in detail at the forces between
nucleons 8
Nuclear forces and the stability of nuclei 9
Comparing the stability of atomic nuclei 11

2 Nuclear fission 16
Discovery of nuclear fission 16
Why does fission occur? 17
Why do fission reactions have to be induced? 18
A closer look at fission products 19
How can fission reactions be started? 20
Using nuclear fission as an energy source 20
Moderators 22
Controlling a thermal reactor 23
Two types of thermal reactor 24
Fast breeder reactors 25
Nuclear fission and the environment 26

3 Nuclear fusion 28
An alternative to nuclear fission 28
The hydrogen (or proton–proton) cycle 30
The carbon cycle 32
Further fusion reactions in stars 33
Achieving nuclear fusion on Earth 33
How plasma is confined 35
Prospects for nuclear fusion as an
energy source 37

4 The search for fundamental particles 40
The idea of fundamental particles 40
Atoms 40

Protons, neutrons and electrons 41
Particles galore 42
Why there are only two types of hadron
in ordinary matter 45
'Who ordered that?' 45

5 Creating and detecting particles 47
How particles can appear from nowhere 47
Choosing appropriate units for the energy
and mass of particles 48
Obtaining particle traces 49
Interpreting particle traces 51

6 Particle accelerators 54
How particles can be accelerated 54
Linear accelerators (Linacs) 55
The cyclotron 56
The synchrotron 59
Fixed targets versus colliding beams 60

7 Making sense of hadrons 64
Finding patterns in hadron reactions 64
Explaining the patterns in hadron reactions 67
Direct experimental evidence for the
quark model 70
Extending the quark model 71
Are quarks fundamental particles? 71

8 Completing the picture 73
Leptons 73
Summary of fundamental particles 75
A fourth fundamental force 75
Baryon decays 75
Beta decay 77
Proton decay 78
Postscript 79

Appendix: Data about particles 81
Answers to questions 82
Glossary of key terms and units 91
Index 92

Introduction

Cambridge Advanced Sciences

The *Cambridge Advanced Sciences* series has been developed to meet the demands of all the new AS and A level science examinations. In particular, it has been endorsed by OCR as providing complete coverage of their specifications. The AS material is presented as a single text for each of biology, chemistry and physics. Material for the A2 year comprises six books in each subject: one of core material and one for each option. Some material has been drawn from the existing *Cambridge Modular Sciences* books; however, many parts are entirely new.

During the development of this series, the opportunity has been taken to improve the design, and a complete and thorough new writing and editing process has been applied. Much more material is now presented in colour. Although the existing *Cambridge Modular Sciences* texts do cover most of the new specifications, the *Cambridge Advanced Sciences* books cover every OCR learning objective in detail. They are the key to success in the new AS and A level examinations.

OCR is one of the three unitary awarding bodies offering the full range of academic and vocational qualifications in the UK. For full details of the new specifications, please contact OCR:

OCR, 1 Hills Rd, Cambridge CB1 2EU
Tel: 01223 553311

The presentation of units

You will find that the books in this series use a bracketed convention in the presentation of units within tables and on graph axes. For example, ionisation energies of $1000\,kJ\,mol^{-1}$ and $2000\,kJ\,mol^{-1}$ will be represented in this way:

Measurement	Ionisation energy $(kJ\,mol^{-1})$
1	1000
2	2000

OCR examination papers use the solidus as a convention, thus:

Measurement	Ionisation energy / $kJ\,mol^{-1}$
1	1000
2	2000

Nuclear and particle physics – an A2 option text

Nuclear and particle physics contains everything needed to cover the A2 option module of the same name. Matters not explicitly mentioned by this syllabus have however sometimes been included where these are needed to provide a more coherent story-line and/or where they are likely to engage/maintain students' interest. For example, a brief consideration of how traces of fast-moving submicroscopic particles can be obtained and of how these traces can be interpreted has been included in the story (chapter 5).

Much of section 5.4.11, 'The nuclear atom', from Module D of the OCR syllabus, is not merely *incidentally relevant* to chapters 1–3 of this book but comprises rather the *essential foundation* to it. It is important that these chapters are fully intelligible in their own right. Many of the very basic ideas from the earlier module have, therefore, been included in a brief introductory section to chapter 1, albeit more briefly than if students were meeting them for the first time. Other, more incidental, ideas from earlier modules are briefly recapitulated, whenever they are needed, at appropriate points in the text.

The two main sections of the book, chapters 1–3 (nuclear physics) and chapters 4–8 (particle physics), have been written so that they may be studied in either order, i.e. as two independent, self-contained stories. This has entailed a certain amount of repetition, but the repetition is not extensive and, because of the different context, can justifiably be regarded as useful consolidation rather than *mere* repetition.

CHAPTER 1

The structure of the nucleus

By the end of this chapter you should be able to:

1 recall that the nuclei of atoms consist of smaller particles called nucleons (protons and neutrons);

2 recall that radioactive decay, nuclear fission and nuclear fusion all involve changes to the nuclei of atoms;

3 interpret and construct nuclear equations using symbols for atomic nuclei and subatomic particles with superscripts/subscripts for nucleon (mass) numbers (A), proton (atomic) numbers (Z) and electrical charges;

4 sketch and interpret a graph showing how the radius of an atomic nucleus varies with the number of nucleons it contains (A);

5 calculate the radius r of a nucleus using the relationship $r = r_0 A^{1/3}$, where r_0 is the radius of a hydrogen-1 nucleus;

6 estimate the density of nuclear matter;

7 use Coulomb's law to determine the electrostatic force of repulsion, and Newton's law to determine the gravitational force of attraction between two adjacent protons, and hence appreciate the need for a short-range attractive force between nucleons holding atomic nuclei together;

8 recall the nature of the strong force (interaction) between nucleons, and sketch and interpret a graphical representation of how this varies with the distance between nucleons;

9 appreciate that the stability of nuclei depends on the balance between attractive and repulsive forces between nucleons;

10 understand the concept of binding energy and appreciate the relationship between binding energy and stability.

Nuclear structure and nuclear reactions: a review of basic ideas

You have already looked at the basic structure of atomic nuclei and at various types of nuclear reaction – nuclear fission, nuclear fusion and radioactive decay – in an earlier module. Before looking in more detail at how and why these nuclear reactions occur, you may find it helpful to be briefly reminded about some basic ideas from that earlier module.

Atomic structure

An atom consists of a small, dense **nucleus** that makes up almost all of the mass of the atom.

Surrounding the nucleus is a much larger volume of space. **Electrons**, which have a negative electrical charge $-e$ but very little mass, move about in this space.

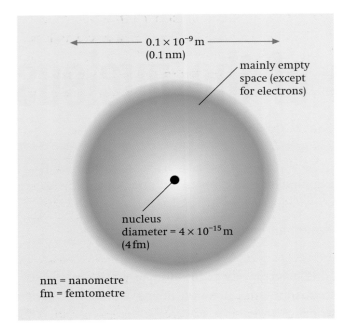

nm = nanometre
fm = femtometre

A typical atom.

SAQ 1.1

What fraction of the diameter of the atom shown in the above diagram is the diameter of its nucleus?

Atomic nuclei are themselves made up of smaller particles called **nucleons**. There are two types of nucleon:

	Mass (u)*	Charge
proton	about 1	$+e$
neutron	about 1	0

[*See *box 1A* on page 4 for an explanation of this unit of mass.]

The diagram below shows the nucleus of a helium atom.

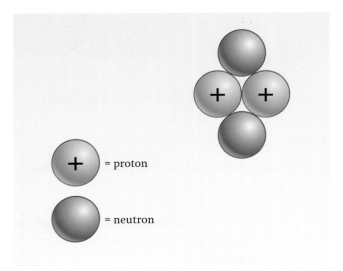

= proton

= neutron

A convenient way of representing the nucleus of this atoms is as follows:

> This is the mass or nucleon number (A) (the total number of nucleons)
>
> This is the atomic or proton number (Z) (the number of protons)
>
> $_{2}^{4}\text{He}$

All the atoms of a particular element have the same number of protons so all the atoms of that element have the same value for Z.

Atoms of the same element may, however, have different numbers of neutrons and so have different values for A. Different kinds of atom of the same element are called **nuclides** (or isotopes) of that element. For example, the commonest type of carbon atom is $_{6}^{12}\text{C}$, but another type of carbon atom is $_{6}^{14}\text{C}$.

Since the nucleon number of an atom tells you the total number of nucleons in its nucleus, the number of neutrons in an atom can be worked out using the relationship:

> neutrons = nucleons − protons
>
> i.e. $N = A - Z$

SAQ 1.2

a In what way are the nuclei of $_{6}^{12}\text{C}$ and $_{6}^{14}\text{C}$ the same?

b In what way are they different?

Atoms have no overall electrical charge. The positive charges of the protons in the nucleus are exactly balanced by an equal number of electrons in the space surrounding the nucleus. The number of electrons in atoms and the way that these electrons are arranged in energy levels, or shells, determines the way that they combine with different atoms in **chemical reactions**.

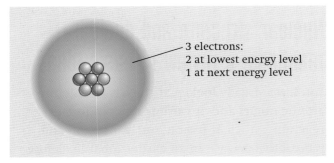

3 electrons:
2 at lowest energy level
1 at next energy level

A $_{3}^{7}\text{Li}$ atom. *Note*: the nucleons are not to the same scale as the electron cloud.

The nuclei of atoms can change, or be made to change, in various ways. Changes to the nuclei of atoms are called **nuclear reactions**. Three important types of nuclear reaction are:

- **radioactive decay**;
- **nuclear fission**;
- **nuclear fusion**.

Radioactive decay

Radioactive decay occurs when the unstable nucleus of an atom *spontaneously* changes into a different nuclide, emitting radiation as it does so. Because it emits radiation, the original unstable nucleus is called a **radionuclide**.

For example:

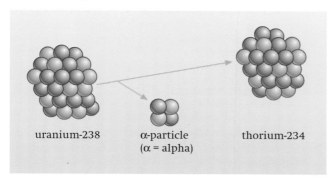

| uranium-238 | α-particle (α = alpha) | thorium-234 |

This decay can be described using a nuclear equation:

$$^{238}_{92}U \rightarrow {}^{4}_{2}He + {}^{234}_{90}Th$$

Notice that the totals of the A numbers and of the Z numbers for the products of this reaction are exactly the same as the A and Z numbers of the original radionuclide. In other words, the A and Z numbers on each side of the nuclear equation *balance*.

$^{14}_{6}C$ is a radionuclide. It decays as shown below:

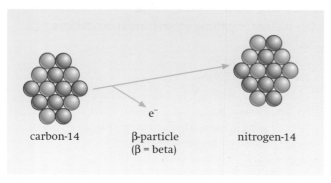

| carbon-14 | β-particle (β = beta) | nitrogen-14 |

The nuclear equation for this decay is:

$$^{14}_{6}C \rightarrow {}^{0}_{-1}e + {}^{14}_{7}N$$

Notice that because the electron (the β-particle) has hardly any mass compared to a nucleon, it is given a mass (nucleon) number of zero. Also because the electron has the opposite electrical charge to a proton it is given a proton number of −1. This means that the A and Z numbers on both sides of the nuclear equation still balance.

SAQ 1.3
The chemical reactions of $^{12}_{6}C$ and $^{14}_{6}C$ are the same but only one isotope is radioactive. Suggest why.

SAQ 1.4
a Give another name for (i) an α-particle, and (ii) a β-particle.
b Describe, in terms of protons, neutrons and electrons, what happens to the nucleus of a carbon-14 atom when it decays.

Nuclear fission

Nuclear fission occurs when a large atomic nucleus splits into two smaller nuclei. This can happen spontaneously but is usually **induced** by bombarding atomic nuclei with neutrons.

For example:

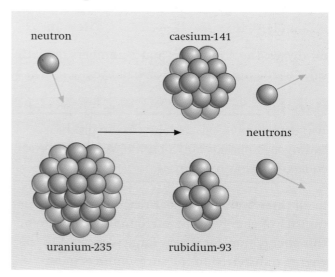

neutron	caesium-141
	neutrons
uranium-235	rubidium-93

This fission can be shown as a nuclear equation:

$$^{235}_{92}U + {}^{1}_{0}n \rightarrow {}^{141}_{55}Cs + {}^{?}_{?}Rb + 2{}^{1}_{0}n$$

Notice that since neutrons are not protons and, unlike electrons, have no electrical charge, they have a Z number of zero.

SAQ 1.5

Calculate, from the previous nuclear equation, the nucleon number (A) and the proton number (Z) of the rubidium atom.

Nuclear fusion

Nuclear fusion occurs when two smaller atomic nuclei join together (fuse) to make a single, larger nucleus. This can occur only when the nuclei which are to fuse have very high energies (i.e. are at a very high temperature).

For example:

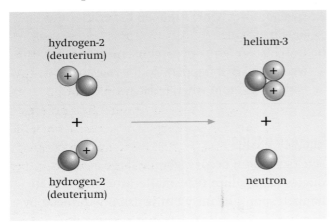

hydrogen-2 (deuterium)

helium-3

+

+

hydrogen-2 (deuterium)

neutron

This fusion can be shown as a nuclear equation:

$$^{2}_{1}H + ^{2}_{1}H \rightarrow ^{3}_{2}He + ^{1}_{0}n$$

As always, the A numbers and Z numbers on both sides of the nuclear equation balance.

SAQ 1.6

Two deuterium nuclei can also fuse to produce a hydrogen-3 nucleus and a proton. Write a nuclear equation for this reaction.

In all three types of nuclear reaction there is a net transfer of energy to the surroundings. Per atom, this energy transfer is very large compared to the energy transferred to the surroundings in an exothermic *chemical* reaction such as burning hydrogen. The transfer of energy to the surroundings during a nuclear reaction involves a loss of mass by the atomic nuclei themselves (see *box 1A*).

The fact that the nuclei produced by nuclear reactions have less mass/energy than the reacting nuclei makes them more stable. The situation is similar to that of a book which has fallen from a shelf to the floor: it then has less gravitational potential energy but is in a more stable position. In order to reverse a nuclear reaction we would need to supply energy, just as we would to put the book back on its shelf. Because the energy that is

---

Box 1A Units and formulae

You will have met all the following pieces of information in earlier modules. You will, however, find them useful (e.g. for calculations) at many points in this book.

For convenience, the very small masses of atoms, atomic nuclei and nucleons are often given in **unified atomic mass units** (u). This unit is based on the mass of an atom of $^{12}_{6}C$, which is defined as having a mass of exactly 12 u.

The mass of each proton and neutron is therefore approximately 1 u. It should, however, be noted that:

- the mass of an isolated neutron or proton is slightly greater than 1 u;
- the mass of an isolated neutron is slightly greater than the mass of an isolated proton;
- the masses of neutrons and protons within atomic nuclei are less than the total of the separate masses of the protons and neutrons they contain. (The difference in mass is a measure of the binding energy of the nucleus.)

	Mass (u)	Mass (kg $\times 10^{-27}$)
proton	1.0073	1.673
neutron	1.0086	1.675

The electrical charge on an electron ($-e$) is -1.602×10^{-19} C (coulomb).

When this charge moves through a potential difference of 1 V (volt) the amount of work done (energy transferred) is 1.602×10^{-19} J (joules).

This very small amount of energy is also called an **electron-volt (eV)**. It is a convenient unit of energy to use when considering nuclear reactions:

$$1 \text{ eV} = 1.602 \times 10^{-19} \text{ J} \approx 1.6 \times 10^{-19} \text{ J}$$

Occasionally, slightly larger units are more convenient, such as:

$$1 \text{ keV} = 1 \times 10^{3} \text{ eV}$$
$$1 \text{ MeV} = 1 \times 10^{6} \text{ eV}$$

A transfer of energy, ΔE, is always accompanied by a change in mass, Δm.

The change in mass which accompanies a transfer of energy is given by the relationship:

$$\Delta E = \Delta m c^{2}$$

where c is the speed of light (2.998×10^{8} m s^{-1}).

Using this relationship, it can be shown that:

$$1 \text{ u} = 931.5 \text{ MeV}$$

Box 1A continued

SAQ 1.7
a   Calculate the energy equivalent, in J, of 1 kg of mass.
b   How does your answer to **a** compare with the 5×10^7 J of chemical energy released by burning 1 kg of petrol?
c   Use your result from **a** to calculate the energy equivalent, in J, of 1 u of mass.
d   Convert your answer to **c** into eV.
e   Express your answer to **d** in MeV.
f   Express your answer to **e** as a round figure.

SAQ 1.8
A thorium-232 nucleus decays to a radium-228 nucleus by emitting an α-particle. The energy released by the decay is 4.08 MeV.

The mass of a thorium-232 nucleus is 232.038 u and the mass of an α-particle is 4.003 u.

Calculate the mass of a radium-228 atom.

lost by nucleons in a nuclear reaction would have to be supplied to make the nucleons move back to their original, less stable position, we can regard the lost energy as *holding* the nucleons in the more stable position. This is why physicists say that the **binding energy** of the nucleons is greater at the end of a nuclear reaction than it was at the start. This idea is explained in more detail on pages 11–13.

The review of basic ideas about nuclear structure and nuclear reactions is now complete. We next need to develop these ideas further so that we can explain more fully what is happening in nuclear reactions and why such reactions happen (or don't happen). In order to do this we first need to consider the forces that act between the nucleons from which atomic nuclei are made.

What force holds atomic nuclei together?

There is no problem in understanding why the electrons in an atom do not escape from the space surrounding the nucleus. There is an **electrostatic**

(**Coulomb**) **force** of attraction between the positively charged nucleus and the negatively charged electrons (see page 27 of *Physics 2*). (What *does* need to be explained is why the electrons do not simply spiral into the nucleus.)

There is, however, a very serious problem with the simple model of an atomic nucleus. The nucleons inside an atomic nucleus are either positively charged protons or electrically neutral neutrons. Electrical forces cannot, therefore, explain how the nucleons in a nucleus are held together. Indeed, because the Coulomb force between protons is a *repulsive* force, we need to explain why such forces don't blow atomic nuclei apart.

This isn't a problem at all, of course, for the nucleus of an ordinary hydrogen atom because this consists of just a single proton (*figure 1.1*). The nuclei of all other elements, however, contain two or more protons and the same number of neutrons or slightly more neutrons than protons. Since there are forces of *repulsion* between each of the protons in these nuclei, there must be some other force acting between nucleons and *attracting* them to each other.

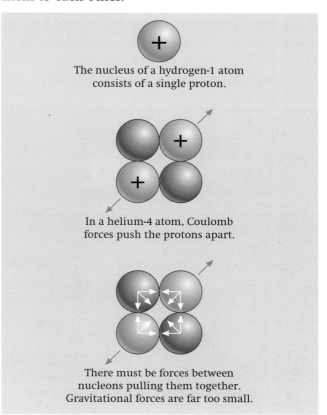

The nucleus of a hydrogen-1 atom consists of a single proton.

In a helium-4 atom, Coulomb forces push the protons apart.

There must be forces between nucleons pulling them together. Gravitational forces are far too small.

● **Figure 1.1** What force holds atomic nuclei together?

SAQ 1.9

As well as hydrogen-1 atoms, there are the isotopes hydrogen-2 (also called deuterium) and hydrogen-3 (also called tritium).

a What nucleons do the nuclei of these isotopes contain?

b Why do the nucleons inside the nuclei of these atoms have no tendency to fly apart?

There will, of course, be a **gravitational force** of attraction between nucleons just as there is between any bodies that have mass. The size of such gravitational forces is, however, far too small to balance the electrostatic forces of repulsion. In fact, as we shall see later, gravitational forces are 10^{36} (i.e. a million million million million million million) times too small!

So some other force of attraction between nucleons must also be acting. This force, which acts between two protons, between two neutrons or between a proton and a neutron, is called the **strong force**.

To understand more about this strong force and to be able to calculate the sizes of the various forces that act between the nucleons inside an atomic nucleus, we need information about the sizes of nucleons and the distances between them. We can obtain this information by measuring the radii of atomic nuclei.

SAQ 1.10

Assuming that nucleons are all the same size, with radius r, and are tightly packed, what distance apart will they be (measured between their centres)?

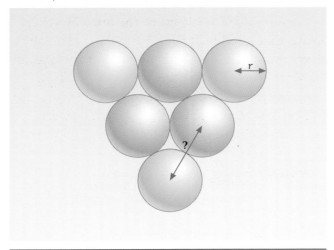

The radii of atomic nuclei

We can't measure the radius of an atomic nucleus directly in the way that we can measure the radius of, for example, a tennis ball (see box 1B). There are, however, ways in which it can be done.

> **Box 1B Problems in measuring the radius of an atomic nucleus**
> - An atomic nucleus doesn't have definite edges. Rather like the Earth's atmosphere, it doesn't suddenly stop but just very gradually fades away.
> - An atomic nucleus is far too small to affect light waves. We can, however, explore its edges by using other methods, such as the scattering (diffraction) of high-energy beams of electrons (see chapter 12 of *Physics 2*).
> - Different methods of measuring the radii of atomic nuclei give results which can differ by up to 50%.

If we measure the nuclear radii r of various different atoms we can then plot these values against the number of nucleons A in each nucleus (*figure 1.2*).

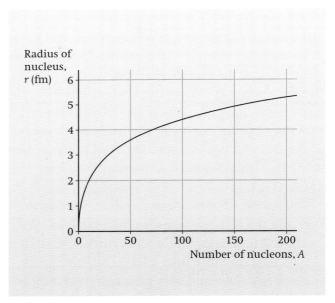

● **Figure 1.2** How the radius of an atomic nucleus varies with the number of nucleons it contains. Note: 1 fm (femtometre) = 10^{-15} m.

SAQ 1.11

a Use the graph in *figure 1.2* to find the value of r when A is 50, 100 and 200.

b Describe the effect on r of doubling the value of A.

As we would expect, the nuclear radius increases with the number of nucleons. The relationship is not proportional, however: the radius increases much more slowly than the number of nucleons. The following diagram shows why.

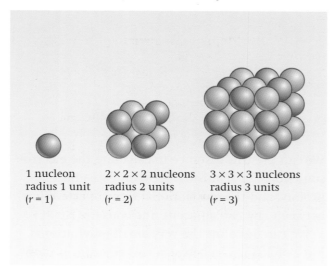

1 nucleon
radius 1 unit
(r = 1)

2 × 2 × 2 nucleons
radius 2 units
(r = 2)

3 × 3 × 3 nucleons
radius 3 units
(r = 3)

From the diagram, you can see that the number of nucleons (A) increases in proportion to the *cube* of the radius:

$$A \propto r^3$$

Putting this the other way round, we can say that the radius of a nucleus is proportional to the *cube root* of the number of nucleons:

$$r \propto A^{1/3}$$

So:

$$r = kA^{1/3}$$

where k is a constant.

If we call the radius of a single nucleon r_0, then a hydrogen atom (A = 1, a single proton) has this radius. So we can write:

$$r_0 = k1^{1/3}$$

So:

$$r_0 = k$$

This means that we can rewrite the general equation as:

$$r = r_0 A^{1/3}$$

Plotting a graph of r against $A^{1/3}$ should therefore give a straight line through the origin (*figure 1.3*).

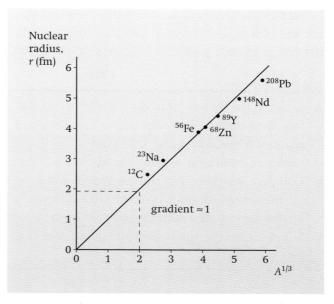

● **Figure 1.3** Plotting r against $A^{1/3}$.

Furthermore, the gradient of this line will be r_0, and will give a value for the radius of a proton:

gradient of graph = $r_0 \approx 1$

∴ radius of hydrogen nucleus (proton) ≈ 1 fm

SAQ 1.12
The line drawn on the graph in *figure 1.3* is *not* the line of best fit through the *plotted* values. Explain why.

The density of nuclear matter

The relationship between the number of nucleons and their volume is very close to being proportional. This strongly suggests that the size and the spacing of the nucleons in an atomic nucleus is – as we had earlier assumed – hardly affected at all by the number of nucleons in the nucleus. It also means that the **density** of all atomic nuclei will be very similar and will, in fact, be similar to the density of the individual nucleons themselves.

We know the mass m of nucleons, so we can use their radius r to calculate their density ρ using the relationship:

$$\text{density} = \frac{\text{mass}}{\text{volume}}$$

$$\rho = \frac{m}{\frac{4}{3}\pi r^3}$$

[since $\frac{4}{3}\pi r^3$ is the volume of a sphere, radius r].

Because nucleons in atomic nuclei are tightly packed this will also give a good indication of the density of atomic nuclei.

SAQ 1.13

a Estimate the density of nuclear matter using the following data:

mass of a nucleon $\cong 1.67 \times 10^{-27}$ kg

radius of a nucleon $\cong 1$ fm $(1 \times 10^{-15}$ m$)$

b Compare the density of nuclear matter with:
   (i) the density of solids on Earth $(10^3-10^4$ kg m$^{-3})$;
   (ii) the density of a neutron star $(10^{17}$ kg m$^{-3})$.

c Suggest how the similarities and differences can be explained.

Looking in detail at the forces between nucleons

Since the nucleons inside an atomic nucleus appear to be tightly packed, the distance between the centres of adjacent nucleons will be the sum of their radii, i.e. about 2 fm.

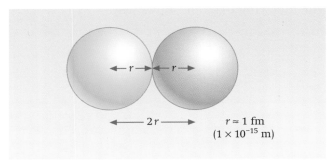

We can use this distance to calculate the electrostatic force of repulsion between two adjacent protons and the gravitational force of attraction between any two adjacent nucleons (see box 1C).

We can discount the very small gravitational force of attraction between two adjacent protons. So there must be some other force of attraction between them acting in the opposite direction to the electrostatic force of repulsion between them. As indicated earlier, this force is called the strong force.

We also know that the radii of nucleons and the distance between adjacent nucleons are not affected by the size of the nucleus that they are in. This means that the strong force must become a *repulsive* force as soon as the nucleons begin to 'overlap', i.e. when the centres of adjacent nucleons become closer than the sum of their radii by even a small amount.

Furthermore, the strong force is different from both the electrostatic and gravitational forces in that it seems to have hardly any effect outside of the nucleus itself. In other words, it is a very *short-range* force. The influence of the strong force extends very little further than the diameter of a single nucleon.

The strong force between two nucleons varies with the distance between the centres of the two nucleons as shown on the graph (*figure 1.4*).

Box 1C Calculating electrostatic and gravitational forces

The electrostatic or Coulomb force F, measured in newtons, between two bodies whose centres are separated by distance r, measured in metres, and which have charges of Q_1 and Q_2, measured in coulombs, is given by:

$$F = \frac{1}{4\pi\varepsilon_0}\frac{Q_1Q_2}{r^2}$$

where ε_0 is a constant called the permittivity of free space with the value 8.85×10^{-12} F m^{-1} (farad per metre).

The gravitational force F, measured in newtons, between two bodies with centres separated by distance r, measured in metres, and which have masses of m_1 and m_2, measured in kilograms, is given by:

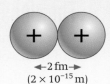

←2 fm→
$(2 \times 10^{-15}$ m$)$

$$F = G\frac{m_1m_2}{r^2}$$

where G is the universal gravitational constant with the value 6.673×10^{-11} N m^2 kg^{-2}.

SAQ 1.14

Use the above formulae, together with the data in *box 1A*, to calculate:

a the Coulomb force of repulsion between two adjacent protons;

b the gravitational force of attraction between two adjacent nucleons;

c the ratio of your answers to **a** and **b**.

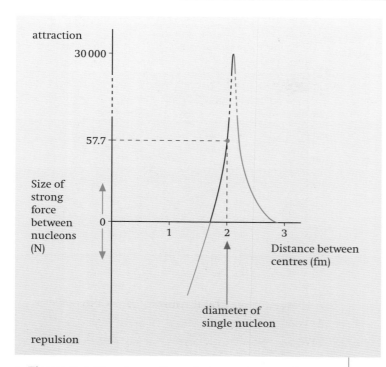

● **Figure 1.4** The strong force between two nucleons.

SAQ 1.15

Explain the significance of the red point and the regions marked green and yellow on the graph in *figure 1.4*.

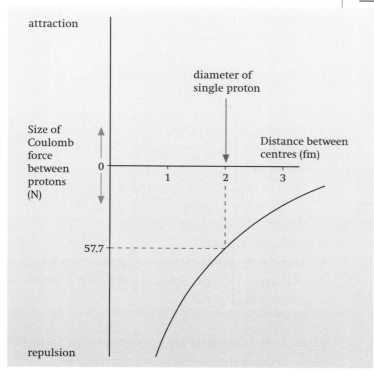

● **Figure 1.5** The electrostatic (Coulomb) force between two protons.

The graph in *figure 1.5* shows how the electrostatic (Coulomb) force of repulsion between two protons varies with the distance between them.

The net force between two protons at any given distance is the difference between the electrostatic force and the strong force. These two forces are balanced when the centres of the protons are separated by a distance equal to the sum of their radii.

SAQ 1.16

a Sketch on the same axes, but using different colours, graphs of the electrostatic force and the strong force between two protons against the distance apart of their centres.

b Still on the same axes, and using a third colour, sketch a graph of the net force between the two protons.

c Describe what the third graph indicates about the net force between two protons and explain the effect this net force will have on the protons when the distance between their centres is: (i) less than 2 fm; (ii) 2 fm; (iii) just over 2 fm; (iv) well over 2 fm.

When the nucleons in a nucleus are packed tightly together, the electrostatic forces of repulsion between protons which are tending to force the protons apart are balanced by the strong force of attraction between adjacent nucleons.

Nuclear forces and the stability of nuclei

Apart from the nuclei of hydrogen-1 atoms, atomic nuclei comprise mixtures of protons and neutrons. There is a very delicate balance between the forces that act on these nucleons inside atomic nuclei: the subtle interplay between the strong forces that act between adjacent nucleons and the electrostatic forces that act between protons determines how stable (or how unstable) a particular nucleus is.

In relatively light nuclei with up to about 40 nucleons (i.e. $A \leq 40$), the strong forces and the electrostatic forces acting on protons balance; the nuclei are stable, provided that the number of protons and neutrons in the nucleus are approximately equal.

Heavy nuclei, however, are stable only if there are more neutrons in the nucleus than there are protons. To understand why, we need to consider the forces that are acting on the protons that are most likely to become detached from a nucleus, i.e. the protons on the outer edge of the nucleus.

As the size of a nucleus increases, the number of protons contributing to the electrostatic force of repulsion on a proton at the edge of the nucleus also increases. This happens because although the electrostatic force decreases in proportion with the square of the distance between protons, it is still quite significant between protons that are at most only a few diameters apart. The number of nucleons contributing to the strong force of attraction acting on the proton, however, remains the same. This is because the strong force falls away very rapidly with distance so that it only acts to any significant extent between adjacent nucleons. To restore the balance between these opposing forces in larger nuclei, additional neutrons are needed. These neutrons increase the distance between protons and so reduce the electrostatic force of repulsion between them.

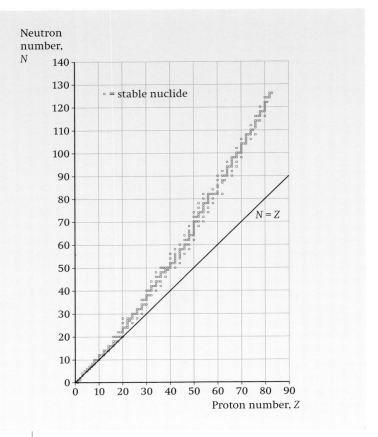

● **Figure 1.6** A plot of N against Z for stable atomic nuclei.

The progressive increase in the ratio of neutrons to protons in stable atomic nuclei, as the size of the nucleus increases, shows up clearly by plotting the number of neutrons (N) against the number of protons (Z) on a graph (*figure 1.6*).

SAQ 1.17

The following are the commonest isotopes of some elements. All of the isotopes are stable.

$^{23}_{11}\text{Na}$ $^{24}_{12}\text{Mg}$ $^{40}_{20}\text{Ca}$ $^{56}_{26}\text{Fe}$ $^{107}_{47}\text{Ag}$ $^{208}_{82}\text{Pb}$

a Calculate the number of neutrons in each nucleus.
b Calculate the neutron:proton ratio in each nucleus.
c What patterns can you see in the neutron:proton ratio?

SAQ 1.18

a Describe, in terms of elements and isotopes, atoms with the same value of Z but different values of N.
b Up to what value of Z on the $N:Z$ graph is:
  (i) $N \approx Z$, on average, for all stable nuclei;
  (ii) $N \approx Z$ for at least one isotope of the particular element?
c There are naturally occurring atoms with values of Z up to 92. Why are no atoms shown on the graph with $Z > 83$?

Many unstable nuclei are known to exist. Some of these occur naturally; others are produced artificially, e.g. in nuclear reactors. The $N:Z$ graph in *figure 1.7* also includes these unstable nuclei.

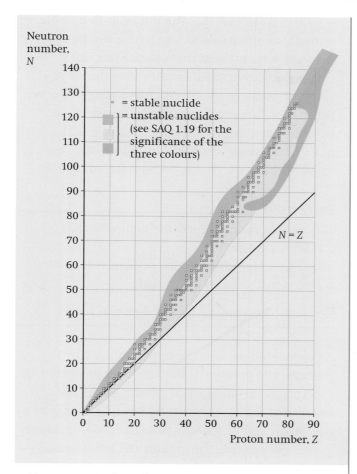

● **Figure 1.7** A plot of N against Z for stable and unstable atomic nuclei.

Unstable nuclei gradually change into more stable nuclei by a process of radioactive decay:

■ An α-particle may be emitted. This reduces the total number of nucleons in the nucleus by 4 and slightly reduces the neutron : proton ratio.

■ A β-particle may be emitted. This alters the neutron : proton ratio without changing the total number of neutrons. When a β⁻-particle (an electron) is emitted, a neutron becomes a proton. Some radioactive substances emit a β⁺-particle (an antielectron, see pages 42 and 43). When this happens, a proton becomes a neutron.

After an α- or β-decay, the nucleus that remains may be in an energetically excited state. The nucleus reaches a more stable (ground) state by emitting one or more bursts (photons) of γ-radiation (γ = gamma). Several α- or β-decays, each of which may be followed by the emission of γ-radiation, may be needed before the nucleus reaches its most stable (ground) state.

SAQ 1.19

a The unstable nuclides on the $N:Z$ plot in *figure 1.7* are shown in three different colours. Which colour corresponds to which type of radioactive decay? Give reasons for your answer.

b The emission of γ-radiation does *not* result in a more stable neutron : proton ratio. Explain why.

It is not possible to predict when any particular nucleus of a radionuclide will decay, so radioactive decay is in this sense a random process. For each radionuclide, however, there is a definite *probability* of any particular nucleus decaying. So in a sample containing many nuclei of a radionuclide, it takes a definite time for *half* of the nuclei to decay. The average time taken for half of the unstable nuclei in a particular sample to decay is known as the **half-life** of that radionuclide. The half-lives of different radionuclides can vary from a very small fraction of a second to billions of years.

Comparing the stability of atomic nuclei

The half-life of an unstable radionuclide gives an indication of its stability: the shorter its half-life, the less stable a particular radionuclide is.

A very useful way of comparing the *relative* stability of *all* atomic nuclei is in terms of their potential energy. The nucleons inside a nucleus tend to stay together because their total potential energy is lower than it would be if they were all separate.

The difference between the potential energy of an atomic nucleus and the total potential energy of all its nucleons if they were separate is called the **binding energy** of the nucleus. This binding energy is the energy released when the nucleons bind together to form the nucleus (see *box 1D* on page 12), though this will not usually have happened in a single step. The same net amount of energy would need to be supplied to unbind the nucleons and produce separate nucleons again.

Einstein showed, in his theory of special relativity, that mass and energy are related by the formula:

$$E = mc^2 \quad \text{or} \quad \Delta E = \Delta m\, c^2$$

Box 1D Binding energy of a deuterium nucleus

Binding energy can be looked at in a number of different ways.

The binding energy of a deuterium nucleus, for example, can be regarded as *any* of the following:
■ the energy released, as γ-radiation, when the nucleus is formed from a proton and a neutron;
■ the energy needed, as γ-radiation, to split the nucleus into its component nucleons;
■ the deficiency in energy/mass of the deuterium nucleus compared to the total energy/mass of a proton and a neutron.

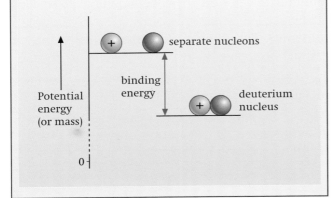

It follows from this that the nucleons in a stable, or semi-stable, nucleus will also have a smaller *mass* than the total mass of the separate nucleons.

[Note: Relativity also implies that the mass of a body increases as its velocity increases. Whenever the mass of a body is mentioned in this book, without anything further being said, it is the mass of the body when stationary, i.e. the **rest mass** of the body, that is being referred to.]

SAQ 1.20

The binding energy of a deuterium nucleus is 2.1 MeV. Calculate:
a the loss in mass when the nucleus is formed;
b the actual mass of the nucleus.

[See *box 1A* on page 4 for the data you need.]

As you would expect, the larger an atomic nucleus, the greater its binding energy (*figure 1.8*).

So far as the stability of atomic nuclei are concerned, however, the total binding energy of a nucleus is less important than the binding energy *per nucleon*. The greater the binding energy per nucleon, the more stable a nucleus is.

A graph of binding energy per nucleon against the number of nucleons (*figure 1.9*) shows several interesting features.

SAQ 1.21

Use *figure 1.9* to answer the following questions.
a Which nucleus is most stable?
b Which three nuclei shown on the graph are more stable than you might expect from the number of their nucleons?
c How might small nuclei become more stable?
d How might large nuclei become more stable?

Comparing the binding energy per nucleon for atomic nuclei of different sizes reveals the intriguing fact that small nuclei and large nuclei are both less stable than nuclei of intermediate sizes, the most stable nucleus of all being the nucleus of ^{56}Fe.

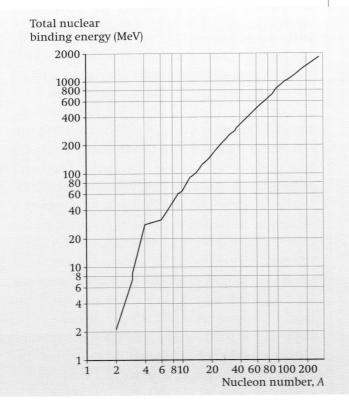

● **Figure 1.8** A plot of binding energy against *A*.
To fit all of the information on to a graph of reasonable size, a *logarithmic* scale is used on each axis. Equal distances along the axes represent equal *ratios*, not equal *distances*.

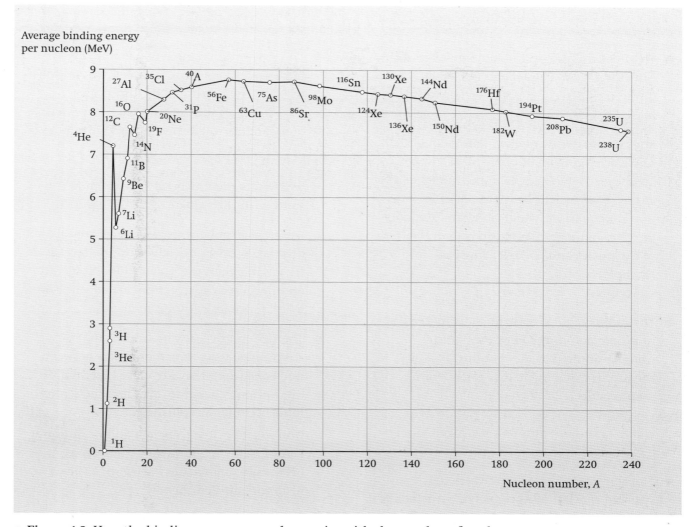

● **Figure 1.9** How the binding energy *per nucleon* varies with the number of nucleons.

It is, therefore, not surprising that very large nuclei are particularly unstable and split up spontaneously in the process we call radioactive decay. We would also expect that:

■ large nuclei could be split into smaller, more stable nuclei;

■ small nuclei could join together to form larger, more stable nuclei.

These processes, which we know as nuclear fission and nuclear fusion, do indeed occur. They are considered in detail in the next two chapters.

SUMMARY

◆ The nuclei of atoms are made up of smaller (subatomic) particles called nucleons (protons: mass 1 u, charge +1; neutrons: mass 1 u, zero charge).

◆ Radioactive decay, nuclear fission and nuclear fusion are all nuclear reactions, i.e. they involve changes to the nuclei of atoms. They can all be represented by nuclear equations which show the symbol, nucleon number (A) and proton number (Z) of the nuclei and particles involved, for example:

^A_Z symbol: ^4_2He ^1_0n

◆ The radius of an atomic nucleus increases in proportion to the cube root of the number of nucleons it contains. That is, the radius r of a nucleus is given by the relationship:

$r = r_0 A^{1/3}$

where r_0 is the radius of a hydrogen atom (i.e. a single proton).

◆ The above relationship indicates that the size and spacing of nucleons in a nucleus is not affected by how many nucleons there are, i.e. that the density of nucleons and nuclei are about the same. The density ρ of a nucleon mass m and radius r can be calculated using the relationship:

$\rho = \dfrac{m}{\frac{4}{3}\pi r^3}$

◆ The electrostatic (Coulomb) force of repulsion F, measured in newtons, between two protons whose centres are separated by distance r, measured in metres, and which have charges of Q_1 and Q_2, measured in coulombs, is given by:

$F = \dfrac{1}{4\pi\varepsilon_0}\dfrac{Q_1 Q_2}{r^2}$

where ε_0 is a constant called the permittivity of free space with the value $8.85 \times 10^{-12}\,\text{F m}^{-1}$ (farad per metre).

◆ The gravitational force of attraction F, measured in newtons, between two protons with centres separated by distance r, measured in metres, and which have masses of m_1 and m_2, measured in kg, is given by:

$F = G\dfrac{m_1 m_2}{r^2}$

where G is the universal gravitational constant with the value $6.673 \times 10^{-11}\,\text{Nm}^2\,\text{kg}^{-2}$.

◆ For adjacent nucleons, whose centres are a distance r_0 apart, the electrostatic force is far greater than the gravitational force, so another force of attraction, called the strong force, must act between nucleons.

◆ The strong force (strong interaction) is a short-range force which only acts between nucleons when they are close together. If the nucleons begin to 'overlap', the strong force becomes a repulsive force.

[You must be able to sketch and/or interpret a graph showing how the strong force between two nucleons varies with the distance between them.]

◆ Nucleons inside a nucleus have less energy than if they were all separate nucleons. This energy difference is called the binding energy of the nucleus.

◆ The binding energy per nucleon of an atomic nucleus is a measure of its stability: the greater the binding energy per nucleon, the more stable the nucleus is.

◆ Changes in energy (ΔE) and mass (Δm) are related by the equation:

$\Delta E = \Delta m\,c^2$

where c is the speed of light ($2.998 \times 10^8\,\text{m s}^{-1}$).

This means that the nucleons inside a nucleus also have less mass than if they were separate nucleons.

Questions

1   The following measurements of nuclear radii were made using X-rays.

Nucleus	^{12}C	^{23}Na	^{56}Fe	^{66}Zn	^{89}Y	^{150}Nd	^{208}Pb
Radius (fm)	3.2	3.8	4.7	5.1	5.4	6.4	7.1

a   Use these figures to plot a graph of r against $A^{1/3}$.

b   Use the graph to find a value for r_0 in the equation:
$$r = r_0 A^{1/3}$$

c   Compare the value of r_0 with that obtained from the graph in *figure 1.3*.

2   Using the $N:Z$ plot in *figure 1.6* and *table 1.1*:

a   identify the element that has the greatest number of stable isotopes;

b   make a list of all the stable nuclides with 20 neutrons.

Proton number	Element	Proton number	Element	Proton number	Element
1	H	33	As	65	Tb
2	He	34	Se	66	Dy
3	Li	35	Br	67	Ho
4	Be	36	Kr	68	Er
5	B	37	Rb	69	Tm
6	C	38	Sr	70	Yb
7	N	39	Y	71	Lu
8	O	40	Zr	72	Hf
9	F	41	Nb	73	Ta
10	Ne	42	Mo	74	W
11	Na	43	Tc	75	Re
12	Mg	44	Ru	76	Os
13	Al	45	Rh	77	Ir
14	Si	46	Pd	78	Pt
15	P	47	Ag	79	Au
16	S	48	Cd	80	Hg
17	Cl	49	In	81	Tl
18	Ar	50	Sn	82	Pb
19	K	51	Sb	83	Bi
20	Ca	52	Te	84	Po
21	Sc	53	I	85	At
22	Ti	54	Xe	86	Rn
23	V	55	Cs	87	Fr
24	Cr	56	Ba	88	Ra
25	Mn	57	La	89	Ac
26	Fe	58	Ce	90	Th
27	Co	59	Pr	91	Pa
28	Ni	60	Nd	92	U
29	Cu	61	Pm	93	Np
30	Zn	62	Sm	94	Pu
31	Ga	63	Eu		
32	Ge	64	Gd		

● **Table 1.1** Proton numbers of elements.

3   Use the information from the graph of binding energy per nucleon against the number of nucleons (*figure 1.9*) to sketch a graph of potential energy per nucleon against the number of nucleons.

CHAPTER 2

Nuclear fission

By the end of this chapter you should be able to:

1 understand what is meant by neutron-induced fission;

2 outline the mechanism of nuclear fission for unstable, massive, neutron-rich nuclei;

3 understand in terms of binding energy, activation energy and excitation energy why fission reactions have to be induced and how neutrons are able to induce them;

4 sketch a graph of how the relative yield of fission products for a fissile material varies with the number of nucleons in the nuclei of those products;

5 estimate, from a graph showing how the binding energy per nucleon varies with the number of nucleons in a nucleus, the energy available from the fission of a uranium-235 nucleus;

6 explain the term 'thermal neutrons' and appreciate the role of moderators in producing these in a nuclear reactor;

7 appreciate the need for the rate of neutron production in a nuclear reactor to be critical (rather than subcritical or supercritical) and describe how this can be achieved;

8 recall that neutrons colliding with uranium nuclei can lead to the production of plutonium-239 without any immediate fission;

9 recall that plutonium-239 is a by-product of nuclear fission reactors, and decays, through the emission of α-particles, with a half-life of over 24 000 years.

Discovery of nuclear fission

Nuclear fission is the splitting of a large atomic nucleus into smaller fragments. It was first discovered in 1938 by Otto Hahn (*figure 2.1*) and Fritz Strassman. They were bombarding uranium-238 atoms with neutrons so that the uranium atoms would capture neutrons and produce atoms of **transuranic elements**, i.e. atoms with a greater proton number (Z) than the largest naturally occurring atoms, uranium (Z = 92).

In their experiments, however, Hahn and Strassman found evidence not only of the transuranic elements that they were trying to make but also of what appeared to be barium atoms (Z = 56). The only possible way that Hahn and Strassman knew about for the atoms of

uranium or transuranic elements to change into barium atoms was by a series of rapid α-particle decays. Since there was no evidence of this, but only of β-particle emission and the normal, very slow α-decay of uranium, Hahn and Strassman concluded that the presence of barium must have been an accident of some kind.

Lise Meitner (*figure 2.1*), a former colleague of Hahn, and Otto Frisch, however, came up with a much bolder explanation. They proposed that neutron bombardment could *split* a uranium-238 nucleus into two smaller nuclei of roughly the same size, each of which then decayed by β-particle emission. They called this neutron-induced splitting process **nuclear fission**.

● **Figure 2.1** Lise Meitner and Otto Hahn.

The ideas of Meitner and Frisch were quickly confirmed, though it turned out that it was in fact uranium-235 (0.7% of natural uranium) rather than uranium-238 (99.3% of natural uranium) which underwent fission:

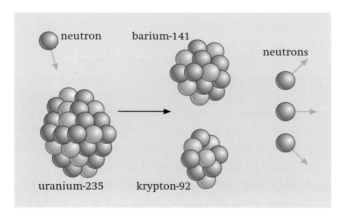

$$\ce{^{1}_{0}n} + \ce{^{235}_{92}U} \longrightarrow \ce{^{141}_{56}Ba} + \ce{^{92}_{36}Kr} + 3\,\ce{^{1}_{0}n}$$

The fission fragments then decay via β-emission to stable atoms, for example:

$$\ce{^{141}_{56}Ba} \xrightarrow{\beta^-} \ce{^{141}_{57}La} \xrightarrow{\beta^-} \ce{^{141}_{58}Ce} \xrightarrow{\beta^-} \ce{^{141}_{59}Pr}\ \text{[stable]}$$

[Note: The β-particles emitted are negatively charged electrons so this type of β-emission is called β⁻-**emission**.]

SAQ 2.1

Write a similar series of nuclear equations for the decay of krypton-92 into stable zirconium-92.

[See *table 1.1* on page 15 for a list of elements and their proton (Z) numbers.]

The fission of each atom of uranium-235 was accompanied by the release of a very large amount of energy compared with the energy released per atom in radioactive decay or the energy released for each bond formed in chemical reactions. Unlike radioactive decay, however, which is spontaneous, fission had to be **induced**, i.e. made to happen. Furthermore, the neutrons released during fission could themselves cause the fission of other nuclei and so produce a **chain reaction**.

Nuclear fission, therefore, provided the possibility of a very powerful source of energy both for peaceful purposes (e.g. generating electricity) and for nuclear bombs.

SAQ 2.2

The average amount of energy released from the fission of a uranium-235 nucleus is about 200 MeV. The average energy released from a single α-decay is about 5 MeV. The energy released per carbon atom when carbon burns is 6.5×10^{-19} J.

How many times more energy is released per atom during the fission of uranium-235:

a than during α-decay;

b than when carbon burns?

[Note: You will find any additional data you need for this question – and other questions in this chapter – in *Box 1A* on page 4.]

Why does fission occur?

As we have seen, when nuclear fission occurs energy is released. This happens because the fission fragments have less potential energy, and less mass, than the larger nucleus which split to produce them.

For example:

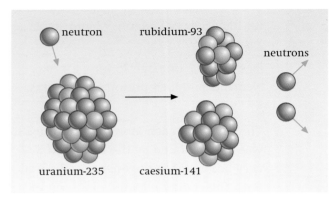

$$^{1}_{0}n + {}^{235}_{92}U \rightarrow {}^{93}_{37}Rb + {}^{141}_{55}Cs + 2{}^{1}_{0}n$$

accurate* masses: 1.01 u   235.04 u   92.92 u   140.92 u   2.02 u

[* For calculating mass changes during nuclear reactions the approximate whole-number masses used to identify isotopes by their A number are not sufficiently accurate.]

SAQ 2.3

Calculate for the above fission reaction:
a the loss of mass (in u);
b the loss of energy (in MeV).

So nuclear fission occurs because it produces atomic nuclei which are energetically more stable than the original atomic nucleus.

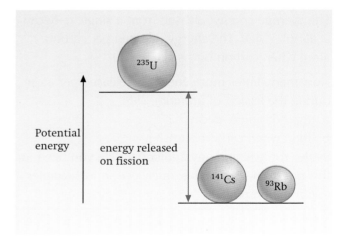

Another way of looking at fission reactions is in terms of **binding energy**. The binding energy per nucleon in each of the fission fragments is greater than the binding energy per nucleon in the original nucleus (*figure 2.2*). So the total binding energy after fission is also greater than it was before.

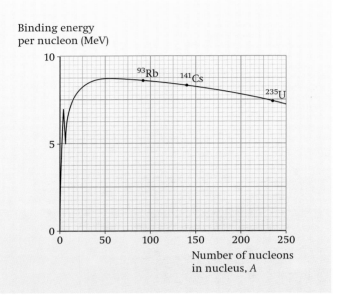

- **Figure 2.2** Binding energy per nucleon for uranium-235 and two of its fission products.

SAQ 2.4

a Use the binding energy graph in *figure 2.2* to estimate the energy transfer/loss in the fission reaction:
   uranium–235 → rubidium–93 + caesium–141
b Compare your answer with the one you obtained by a different method in SAQ 2.3(b).

Why do fission reactions have to be induced?

Though fission reactions result in lower potential energy and more stable nuclei, they don't usually just happen spontaneously. They normally have to be *induced*. To understand why this is so, it is useful to have a model of the nucleus.

The nucleons in atomic nuclei seem to behave in much the same way as the molecules in a drop of water. So scientists use a model of the nucleus called the **liquid drop model**. When a water molecule is in the centre of a drop of water, many forces of attraction act on it in many directions so they tend to cancel each other out. For molecules on the outside of a drop of water, however, there is a net inward force of attraction (*figure 2.3*). There is a similar net inward force acting on the nucleons which are on the outer surface of an atomic

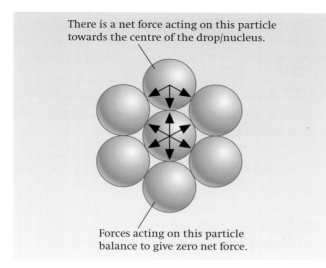

Figure 2.3 The liquid drop model of an atomic nucleus.

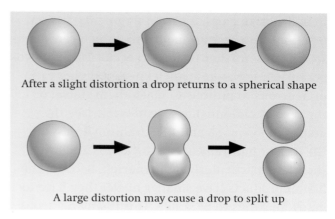

After a slight distortion a drop returns to a spherical shape

A large distortion may cause a drop to split up

● **Figure 2.4** The liquid drop model of nuclear fission.

nucleus. In both cases, the result of the net inward forces on the outer particles is to produce a spherical shape. This shape has less surface area and less potential energy than any other shape that has the same volume.

Though random movement of the particles will cause temporary slight variations, a liquid drop or an atomic nucleus will always tend to return to its most stable, spherical shape (*figure 2.4 top*). If, however, the shape of a liquid drop is distorted too much, it may break up into two smaller droplets (*figure 2.4 bottom*). Each of these droplets quickly assumes the most stable, spherical shape. Similarly, if the shape of an atomic nucleus is distorted far enough it may split up into two smaller nuclei.

To distort an atomic nucleus we need to supply it with energy. In the case of uranium-235, the required energy is produced by the capture of a slow-moving neutron. Nuclear fission then occurs.

A closer look at fission products

So far in this chapter two different pairs of fission fragments resulting from the fission of uranium-235 have been referred to:
■ barium-141 + krypton-92, and
■ caesium-141 + rubidium-93.

In fact there are many different pairs of fission fragments that can result from any fission reaction. *Figure 2.5* shows how common the different fission fragments from the fission of uranium-235 are.

SAQ 2.5

a About what percentage of uranium-235 atoms split into fragments of almost equal size?
b Explain why the right-hand side of the graph (*figure 2.5*) is almost exactly the mirror image of the left-hand side.
c Suggest a reason why certain pairs of fission fragments are much more common than others.

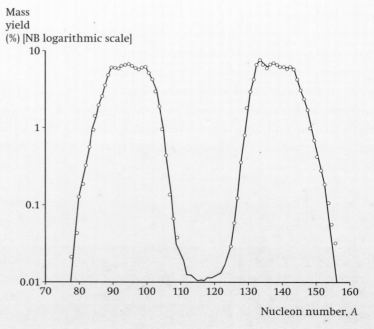

● **Figure 2.5** Fission fragments from the fission of uranium-235.

In addition to pairs of fission fragments, fission reactions also produce neutrons, which can themselves cause further fissions to occur. This happens because larger atomic nuclei need a higher ratio of neutrons to protons to make them stable, or in the case of radionuclides, semi-stable (see the graphs in *figures 1.6* and *1.7*). Uranium atoms are the largest naturally occurring atoms and are, therefore, particularly **neutron-rich**. Because the fission products have smaller nuclei they have too many neutrons to be stable. This is why neutrons are emitted at the instant of fission. Usually, two or three of these **prompt neutrons** are emitted from the fission of each uranium-235 nucleus, the exact number depending on the particular pair of fission fragments. In addition to the prompt neutrons, further neutrons may be emitted following β-decay of the fission fragments. This typically happens within seconds of the original fission and accounts for about 1% of the neutrons released. These **delayed neutrons** are important for the control of fission reactions in nuclear reactors.

How can fission reactions be started?

As we have seen, fission reactions release neutrons which can then cause further fission and so keep the reaction going. However, some *other* source of neutrons is needed to get a fission reaction started in the first place.

One way of supplying these initial neutrons is that used by Hahn and Strassman in their discovery of nuclear fission. The stable isotope beryllium-9 has a relatively loosely bound neutron, with a binding energy of only 1.7 MeV. If a typical 5 MeV α-particle from radioactive decay strikes a beryllium-9 nucleus, a neutron may be released:

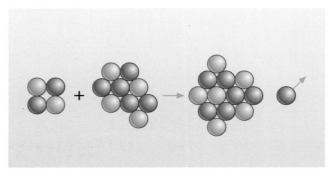

α-particle + beryllium-9 → carbon-12 + neutron

By mixing beryllium-9 and an α-emitter with a long half-life, e.g. radium-226, a mixture that emits neutrons at a steady rate can be produced.

SAQ 2.6

Write a nuclear equation for the reaction between an α-particle and a beryllium-9 nucleus.

Another method of producing neutrons is by using transuranic nuclei that result from bombarding large nuclei with neutrons. Though these transuranic nuclei mainly decay by emitting α-particles, a small percentage decay by **natural fission** (rather than by neutron-induced fission as is needed with uranium). This natural fission releases neutrons.

Nuclei with masses greater than about 280 have zero fission activation energy and are extremely likely to undergo spontaneous natural fission. Any *naturally occurring* nuclei with masses greater than about 250 will also have decayed by spontaneous fission since the formation of the matter which now comprises the Earth. The most massive naturally occurring nuclide, uranium-238, can decay by natural fission, but this is very much less likely than by α-decay. The respective half-lives are 10^{16} years and 4.5×10^9 years.

SAQ 2.7

How many times less likely is the natural fission of uranium-238 than α-decay?

Using nuclear fission as an energy source

In principle, nuclear fission, being a strongly exothermic chain reaction, is a potentially useful energy source. In practice, however, harnessing this energy involves solving many technological problems.

One of the most important of these problems is that of controlling the rate of nuclear fission so that the reaction proceeds continuously without getting out of control. For this to happen, neutrons with energies in exactly the right range must encounter uranium-235 atoms at exactly the right rate.

On average, 2.5 neutrons are released each time a single neutron causes the fission of a uranium-235 atom. It might seem, therefore, that there should be no problem in keeping the reaction going once it has started. In fact, however, there are several reasons why this is not so.

Firstly, some neutrons will be lost from the outside of the reactor. The larger the volume of fissile material in the reactor, the smaller the proportion of neutrons lost in this way. So, once we have taken account of the other factors discussed below, we must make sure that the nuclear reactor is big enough for these lost neutrons not to prevent the reaction from continuing. A mass of fissile material that is large enough for a chain reaction to continue once it has been started is called a **critical mass**.

SAQ 2.8

The diagrams show three different sized cubes of fissile material. Copy the table below and complete it using the information given.

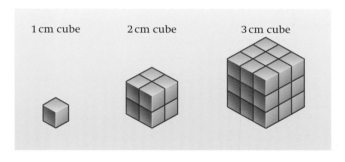

Volume
$1 \times 1 \times 1$ $2 \times 2 \times 2$ $3 \times 3 \times 3$
Surface area
$6 \times 1 \times 1$ $6 \times 2 \times 2$ $6 \times 3 \times 3$

Neutrons capable of causing fission are produced at a rate of 10×10^6 per cm^3 per second inside each cube but are lost at a rate of 4×10^6 per cm^2 per second from the surface of each cube.

Cube side (cm)	Neutrons produced ($10^6 s^{-1}$)	Neutrons lost ($10^6 s^{-1}$)	Sustainable? (Yes or No)
1			
2			
3			

Secondly, only about 0.7% of natural uranium is fissile uranium-235. The remaining 99.3% is the very much less fissile uranium-238. An atom of uranium-238 can, however, capture a neutron to become uranium-239. The loss of neutrons in this way can be reduced by increasing the proportion of uranium-235 in the uranium that is used as fuel. Enriching uranium in this way is, however, a tedious and expensive business.

Thirdly, and most importantly, most of the neutrons emitted during the fission of uranium-235 do not have the energies that most effectively cause the fission of further uranium-235 atoms.

As you can see from *figure 2.6*, neutrons with energies in the 1–2 MeV range are the most numerous. These are known as **fast neutrons**. Fewer than 0.5% of these neutrons cause fission of uranium-235 atoms, because they are too fast. (Fewer than 0.5% of them cause fission of uranium-238 atoms, but the reason this time is that they are too slow!)

Fast neutrons are, in fact, very much more likely to transfer their energy by repeated collisions than they are to cause fission. Alternatively, they may be captured by uranium-238 nuclei to produce uranium-239 (which then decays to plutonium-239 as described on page 25). Such capture is especially likely to happen as neutrons are slowed by repeated collisions and their energies fall to values in the range 6–100 eV.

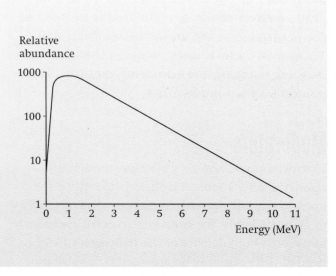

● **Figure 2.6** Energy distribution of neutrons emitted in the neutron-induced fission of uranium-235.

Box 2A Calculating the energy of thermal neutrons

The mean kinetic energy E_k (in joules) of the separate particles in a substance which has a temperature T (kelvin) is given by:

$$E_k = \tfrac{3}{2}kT$$

where k is the Boltzmann constant (1.38×10^{-23} J K^{-1}).

SAQ 2.10

Calculate the kinetic energy, in eV, of a thermal neutron i.e. whose energy is equivalent to a temperature of 400 K (127 °C).

SAQ 2.9

Explain why a chain reaction cannot be maintained in natural uranium metal, no matter how large the piece of metal is.

Neutrons which have energies lower than about 6 eV are far less likely to be captured by uranium-238 atoms. If their energies are reduced still further to *thermal* levels, i.e. the energies the neutrons would have simply because of their temperature, they are then very much more likely to cause fission of uranium-235 nuclei. These slow-moving neutrons with very low energies are known as **thermal neutrons** (see *box 2A* on page 22).

A nuclear reactor which depends on the action of thermal neutrons is called a **thermal reactor**. To produce an operational thermal reactor, we need an effective way of reducing the energies of the neutrons emitted during fission from about 1–2 MeV to thermal levels. while at the same time avoiding too many of them being captured. This process is called **moderation**.

Moderators

Hydrogen nuclei are very effective moderators, requiring only about 18 collisions to reduce the energy of neutrons with initial energies of 1–2 MeV to thermal levels. For collisions to occur frequently, however, a high density of the hydrogen nuclei is needed. This can only be provided by a substance that is in liquid or solid form. Water, each molecule of which contains two hydrogen atoms (plus

one oxygen atom), is a suitable substance (*figure 2.7*). Water has the further benefit that it can also be used for transferring thermal energy from the reactor in order to generate electricity. The main problem with using water as a moderator is that hydrogen atoms do, in fact, capture a significant proportion of neutrons. This means that the fuel needs to have a higher proportion of uranium-235 than the 0.7% found in natural uranium. Increasing this proportion to 2–3% is expensive.

Heavy water, containing hydrogen-2 (deuterium) rather than hydrogen-1, is not quite such an effective moderator, since about 25 collisions are required to reduce the energy of 1–2 MeV neutrons to thermal levels. This is because, the closer the mass of the body a neutron collides with to the mass of the neutron itself, the greater the energy transferred from the neutron to that body. A further problem is caused by the fact that any neutrons which are captured produce hydrogen-3 (tritium) which is radioactive and toxic. Fewer neutrons are, however, captured than with ordinary water, so natural uranium can be used as the fuel.

Another substance that can be used as a moderator is carbon in the form of graphite blocks. This is cheap and easy to handle but carbon atoms

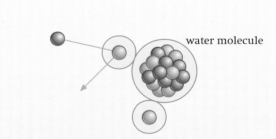

water molecule

Each time a neutron strikes a hydrogen-1 nucleus, it transfers some of its energy.

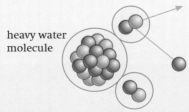

heavy water molecule

With hydrogen-2 nuclei, less energy is transferred on each collision but fewer neutrons are captured.

● **Figure 2.7** Using water and heavy water as moderators.

have an even greater mass so more than 100 collisions are required to reduce the kinetic energy of 1–2 MeV neutrons to thermal levels and graphite also captures neutrons to a significant extent. Furthermore, a separate substance is needed to transfer the thermal energy from the reactor to where it is needed. A gas is normally used for this purpose, for example carbon dioxide.

With appropriate moderation and an appropriate fuel, the necessary 40% of the neutrons released during the fission of uranium-235 will themselves cause further fission so that a chain reaction can be sustained.

SAQ 2.11

Explain why a chain reaction will only occur if at least 40% of the neutrons released by fission of uranium–235 themselves cause further fission.

For a safe thermal reactor, however, we not only need *enough* neutrons of the correct energy to sustain the reaction, but we also need to ensure that there are not *too many* such neutrons, or the reaction will accelerate out of control.

Controlling a thermal reactor

For a nuclear fission reaction to be sustained without getting out of control, just one of the neutrons released from each fission must itself cause a further fission. In other words, the **reproduction factor** of the reactor must be exactly 1. The reaction is then said to be **critical** (*figure 2.8*). When the reproduction factor is less than 1 the reaction is **subcritical**; when the reproduction factor is greater than 1 the reaction is **supercritical**.

Reproduction factors of at least 1 can be produced by using moderators, as described in the previous section, i.e. **criticality** can be achieved. To keep a nuclear reactor *exactly* critical, however, and prevent it from becoming subcritical or supercritical, the number of thermal neutrons needs to be very carefully controlled. This is done using **control rods** made of cadmium or boron steel which are excellent absorbers of thermal neutrons.

If a reactor is in danger of going supercritical, these rods can be lowered into the reactor. If a reactor is becoming subcritical, the control rods are slowly raised until criticality is achieved again.

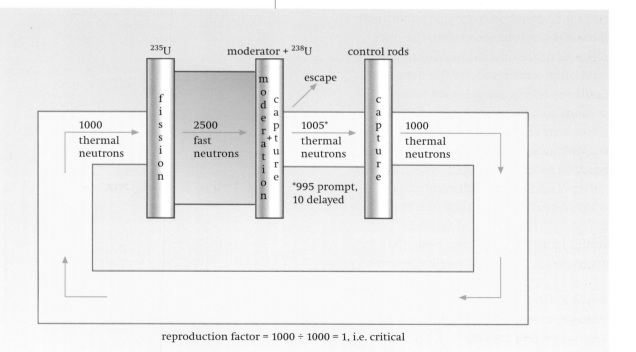

● **Figure 2.8** Neutron flow in a critical thermal reactor.

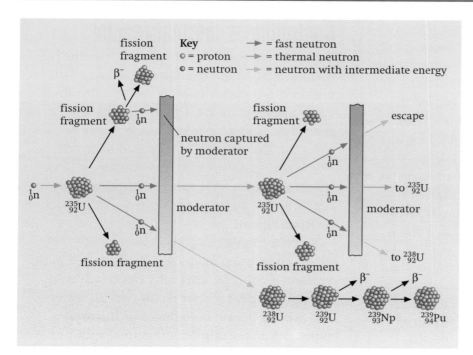

● **Figure 2.9** Summary of the main reactions in a thermal reactor.

Nuclear fission chain reactions can, however, accelerate or decelerate very rapidly. Even with control rods they would be impossible to control if it weren't for the 1% of *delayed* neutrons described earlier (see page 20). The reactor is designed to be just subcritical for the prompt neutrons (i.e. the ones released at the instant of fission) and criticality is achieved via the delayed neutrons which are released a few seconds to a few minutes later. This time delay makes it possible to use control rods to maintain a constant reaction rate.

Figure 2.8 (on page 23) summarises what happens to neutrons in a thermal reactor at criticality and *figure 2.9* summarises the main reactions that occur inside a thermal nuclear reactor.

SAQ 2.12

Describe in words what *figure 2.8* shows. Begin your description:

For every 1000 thermal neutrons that produce fission of uranium-235 atoms …

Two types of thermal nuclear reactor

In addition to a nuclear fuel, a moderator and control rods, a thermal reactor also needs a **coolant** to transfer thermal energy from the core of the reactor to where it is needed (e.g. to produce steam for generating electricity).

Figure 2.10 shows two common types of thermal reactor:
- a pressurised water reactor (developed in the USA);
- a gas-cooled reactor (developed in the UK).

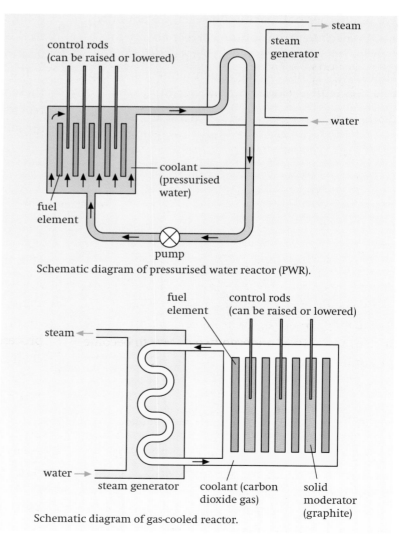

Schematic diagram of pressurised water reactor (PWR).

Schematic diagram of gas-cooled reactor.

● **Figure 2.10** Two common types of thermal reactor.

Box 2B Why a thermal reactor can't explode

People are sometimes worried that if a thermal reactor gets out of control, i.e. becomes supercritical, it might explode like a gigantic nuclear bomb. There is, in fact, no danger at all of this happening, though out-of-control thermal reactors can cause – and occasionally have caused – quite serious accidents in other ways.

To create a nuclear explosion, the rate of fission must accelerate very quickly indeed or, in other words, there must be a very high reproduction rate. Natural uranium, however, contains less than 1% of fissile uranium–235, and uranium that is enriched for use in pressurised water reactors still contains less than 3%. This means that the reproduction rate is much lower than 1, i.e. it is significantly subcritical. Moderators increase the reproduction rate to allow a sustainable reaction, but even if control rods are completely disabled, the reproduction rate would never rise very much higher than 1.

If a thermal reactor were to go supercritical, therefore, its core might overheat sufficiently to melt (and if a graphite moderator was used, to catch fire) but it would not become a nuclear bomb.

To make a fission bomb from uranium, almost pure uranium–235 is needed. With no uranium–238 present to capture neutrons, a 15 kg lump of uranium–235 about the size of a man's fist is big enough to become critical without needing any moderator.

SAQ 2.14

a Explain why a lump of uranium–235 smaller than 15 kg cannot become critical.

b What must be done to a lump of uranium–235 with a mass of more than 15 kg to make it actually achieve criticality?

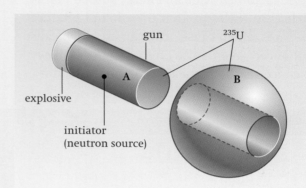

The two sub-critical masses A and B can be bought quickly together (using the explosive) to form a supercritical mass.

SAQ 2.13

For each type of reactor shown in *figure 2.10*:

a name the coolant;

b describe how the neutrons are moderated;

c suggest, with reasons, what fuel is used.

Fast breeder reactors

As we have already seen, uranium-238 nuclei can capture neutrons, especially those with energies in the range 6–100 eV, to produce uranium-239 nuclei. These then undergo two decays to become plutonium-239:

$$^{238}_{92}\text{U} + ^{1}_{0}\text{n} \rightarrow ^{239}_{92}\text{U} \xrightarrow{\ \ \beta^-\ \ } ^{239}_{93}\text{Np} \xrightarrow{\ \ \beta^-\ \ } ^{239}_{94}\text{Pu}$$

Plutonium-239 is radioactive and, although the α-particles it emits are easily shielded, its half-life of 24 000 years and its extreme toxicity inside human bodies make it a very dangerous waste product of thermal reactors.

The plutonium-239 does not, however, need to be wasted. It is itself fissionable, requiring fast neutrons with energies of around 1 MeV to make

this happen. The plutonium-239 produced in thermal reactors can, therefore, be chemically separated out, a much simpler process than physically separating uranium-235 from uranium-238, and used as a nuclear fuel.

Because the fission of plutonium-239 uses fast neutrons, a reactor which uses this fuel is known as a **fast reactor**. On average, 2.91 neutrons are emitted during the fission of each plutonium-239 nucleus. Only one of these is needed to sustain the fission reaction; the others are captured by uranium-238 which surrounds the core. This process actually produces *more* plutonium-239 than is used in the reactor core. Because this type of fast reactor 'breeds' its own fuel it is called a **fast breeder reactor**.

SAQ 2.15

Explain why fast breeder reactors do not need a moderator.

Fast breeder reactors can convert the otherwise wasted 99.3% of natural uranium into useful nuclear fuel. Despite this advantage, however, the detailed technology of fast breeder reactors has proved difficult. There are also ethical and political concerns since the plutonium-239 that is used and 'bred' in fast breeder reactors can also be used directly, without further complex and costly processing, to make fission bombs.

Nuclear fission and the environment

Fission reactors provide an energy source that is very clean in the sense that they do not produce waste gases which cause acid rain or which cause an enhanced greenhouse effect. There are, however, concerns about the risks of radiation, not only because of the emissions of radioactive material from nuclear power stations (especially during accidents) but also from the radioactive wastes, some of which have a long half-life (e.g. 24 000 years for plutonium-239). No one is certain how securely these wastes can be contained. Making provision for their containment and for the decommissioning of nuclear reactors when their useful life is over also adds considerably to the cost of nuclear energy.

Much more promising from the point of view of being safe and environmentally friendly is the use of nuclear *fusion* as a source of energy. This is the subject of the next chapter.

SUMMARY

◆ The splitting of a large, unstable, atomic nucleus into two smaller (but still quite large) fragments is called nuclear fission.

◆ Unlike the decay of radionuclides, which is spontaneous, nuclear fission has to be induced by neutrons.

◆ An unstable nucleus may split in a number of different ways. This means that a particular nuclide may split into many different pairs of fission products.
[You must be able to sketch a graph of how the relative yields of the different products of a given nuclear fission vary with nucleon number.]

◆ Before nuclear fission can occur, neutrons must transfer energy to the unstable nucleus.

◆ Once a fission reaction has been induced, it releases further neutrons, so that fission can continue via a chain reaction.

◆ For a chain reaction to occur, the rate at which neutrons are produced must be at least as great as the rate at which they are lost.

◆ Most of the neutrons released during the fission of uranium-235 are fast, high-energy neutrons. Further fission is most effectively produced by slower moving neutrons with energies corresponding to temperatures of a few hundred degrees celsius. These are called thermal neutrons.

◆ Nuclear reactors which use thermal neutrons to sustain the fission of uranium-235 are called thermal reactors. Moderators, such as graphite or water, are used to reduce the energy of the neutrons produced by fission to thermal levels.

◆ Control rods, containing e.g. boron or cadmium, are used to absorb thermal neutrons so that the rate at which these are produced is critical, i.e. exactly equal to the rate at which they are being lost.

◆ Inside thermal reactors, some of the neutrons colliding with uranium-238 nuclei produce nuclei of plutonium-239. This is a radionuclide which emits α-particles and has a half-life of 24 000 years.

◆ Plutonium-239 does not undergo fission in thermal reactors but can be used in reactors which use fast neutrons. These are called fast reactors.

Questions

1 *A nuclear detective story*
In samples of uranium from most places on Earth, the proportion of uranium-235 is always very similar, i.e. 0.007 20 ± 0.000 01. The half-life of uranium-235 is 7.0×10^8 years. So 2×10^9 years ago the proportion of uranium-235 would have been about 0.05 (5%), i.e. capable of achieving criticality using water as a moderator.

At Oklo, in Gabon, West Africa, the proportion of uranium-235 in samples of uranium varies from 0.000 44 to 0.007 17, i.e. it is significantly lower than in all other known samples.

The table shows the percentage abundance of neodymium isotopes in samples from Oklo, from other parts of the world, and from the products of uranium-235 fission.

Nd isotope							
	142	143	144	145	146	148	150
Oklo	2	24	30	18	15	8	3
Elsewhere	26	11	23	7	18	5	10
^{235}U fission	0	28	26	18	15	10	3

a Suggest how the depletion of uranium-235 in the uranium from Oklo might have happened. Use the information above to support your suggested explanation.

b Suggest one further piece of evidence which, if it could be provided, would help to support your suggestion.

2 The graphs in *figure 2.11* show the relative probabilities of neutrons with different energies causing fission when they strike nuclei of uranium-235 and uranium-238. Comment on the significant features of the graphs.

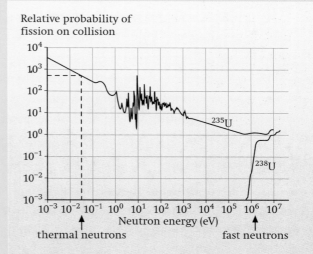

● **Figure 2.11** For question 2.

CHAPTER 3

Nuclear fusion

By the end of this chapter you should be able to:

1 appreciate that, for protons to fuse, electrostatic (Coulomb) forces of repulsion between them must be overcome;

2 understand that, as two positively charged particles approach one another, their electric potential energy increases;

3 apply the concepts of kinetic energy and of electric potential energy to charged particles to explain why high temperatures are required for fusion;

4 use the relationship $E_k = 2 \times 10^{-23} T$ and given values of electric potential energy to determine the temperature required for the fusion of nuclei;

5 explain, from given details, the stages involved in the hydrogen cycle and the carbon cycle;

6 estimate, from a graph showing how binding energy per nucleon varies with the number of nucleons in a nucleus, the energy available from the fusion of hydrogen to form helium;

7 represent and interpret fusion reactions in terms of nuclear equations;

8 describe the conditions under which nuclear fusion occurs in the Sun;

9 outline what is meant by plasma;

10 appreciate that practical fusion reactors are under development and show an awareness of the difficulties involved;

11 recall that the deuterium–tritium (D–T) reaction may be the most likely way of achieving fusion on a practical scale;

12 outline the principles of operation of the prototype (JET) fusion reactor;

13 describe how energy may be extracted from a nuclear fusion reactor;

14 explain why plasma is confined by a gravitational field in the Sun but inertial or magnetic confinement must be used on Earth;

15 describe the possible advantages of nuclear fusion as an energy source.

An alternative to nuclear fission

Figure 3.1 shows a graph of binding energy per nucleon plotted against the number of nucleons in an atomic nucleus (*A*). Notice that the binding energy per nucleon has its maximum value for the nuclei of iron-56 (^{56}Fe). This suggests an alternative to nuclear fission as a nuclear energy source.

Instead of climbing the binding energy curve from the right-hand side via the fission of large atomic nuclei, we could climb it from the left-hand side via the **fusion** of small atomic nuclei. The increase in binding energy resulting from such fusion would show itself in a transfer of energy to the surroundings and a corresponding loss of nuclear mass.

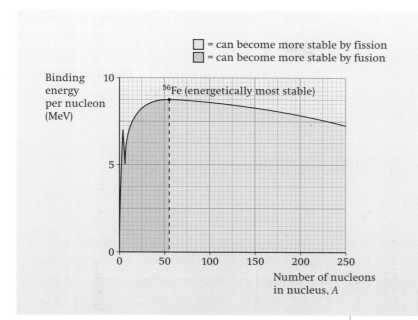

= can become more stable by fission
= can become more stable by fusion

Binding energy per nucleon (MeV)

^{56}Fe (energetically most stable)

Number of nucleons in nucleus, A

● **Figure 3.1** Binding energy per nucleon plotted against the number of nucleons in an atomic nucleus.

The biggest transfer of energy (ΔE) and loss of mass (Δm) from nuclear fission results from the fission of the *largest* atomic nuclei, i.e. uranium. The biggest transfer of energy and loss of mass from nuclear fusion, however, results from the fusion of the *smallest* atomic nuclei, i.e. hydrogen.

SAQ 3.1

How would you expect the energy released per nucleon in the fusion of hydrogen nuclei to compare with the energy released per nucleon in the fission of uranium nuclei? Give reasons for your answer.

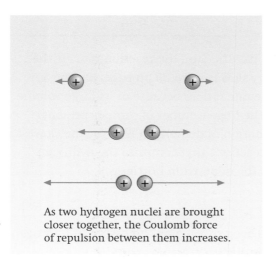

As two hydrogen nuclei are brought closer together, the Coulomb force of repulsion between them increases.

The problem with nuclear fusion reactions, however, is the initial energy that is needed to make them happen. Atomic nuclei carry a positive electrical charge so there is a very strong force of electrical repulsion (Coulomb force) between them.

The atomic nuclei that have the smallest positive charge are hydrogen nuclei. Before two of these nuclei can fuse, they must first do the work that is necessary to overcome the force of repulsion or Coulomb barrier between them. The work that is done to bring two hydrogen nuclei together **increases** their electric potential energy. It is only when the nuclei are close enough together for the strong force to come into play and cause the nuclei to fuse that energy is released. The overall potential energy of the resulting two-proton nucleus then falls to a lower, more stable level. [Note: A two-proton nucleus is unstable so one of the protons changes into a neutron – see page 30.]

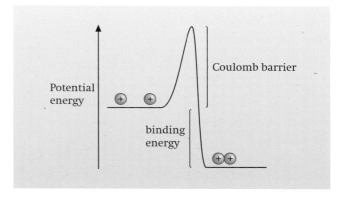

Potential energy

Coulomb barrier

binding energy

For the hydrogen nuclei to have enough kinetic energy to overcome the Coulomb barrier, the hydrogen must be at a very high temperature. Such high temperatures are not normally reached on Earth but they can be found in the core of a star.

Stars such as the Sun comprise mostly hydrogen (about 90%) and helium (about 9%). Some of the hydrogen nuclei in the core of these stars have sufficient energy for fusion to occur. The energy that these stars emit in the form of electromagnetic radiation is released during the conversion of hydrogen nuclei to helium nuclei via a series of nuclear fusion reactions.

Box 3A Calculating the kinetic energy needed for two hydrogen nuclei to fuse

The electrostatic (Coulomb) force F, in newtons, between two bodies with charges Q_1 and Q_2 coulombs at a distance r metres apart is given by:

$$F = \frac{1}{4\pi\varepsilon_0} \frac{Q_1 Q_2}{r^2}$$

where ε_0 is the permittivity of free space, which has the value $8.85 \times 10^{-12}\,\mathrm{F\,m^{-1}}$.

The work which must be done, in joules, to bring the two charged bodies from infinity (i.e. as far apart as they can get) to a distance apart equal to the sum of their radii is given by:

$$\frac{Q_1 Q_2}{4\pi\varepsilon_0 (r_1 + r_2)}$$

where r_1 and r_2 are the radii of the two bodies.

The work that is done on these particles increases their electric potential energy.

The size of the electrical charge on a hydrogen nucleus is e (the same as that on an electron) and the radius of a hydrogen nucleus is r_0:

$$e = 1.6 \times 10^{-19}\,\mathrm{C}$$
$$r_0 \approx 1 \times 10^{-15}\,\mathrm{m}$$

So for fusion to occur, hydrogen nuclei must have kinetic energies given by:

$$\frac{e^2}{4\pi\varepsilon_0 (2r_0)}\ \text{joules}$$

or

$$\frac{e}{4\pi\varepsilon_0 (2r_0)}\ \text{electron-volts}$$

The mean kinetic energy (E_k in joules) of a particle in a population of particles which have a temperature T (kelvin) is given by:

$$E_k = \tfrac{3}{2}kT$$

where k is the Boltzmann constant ($1.38 \times 10^{-23}\,\mathrm{J\,K^{-1}}$).

SAQ 3.2

a Calculate the kinetic energy needed to bring two hydrogen nuclei close enough to fuse: (i) in joules; (ii) in MeV.

b Calculate the temperature at which hydrogen nuclei will, on average, have the required energy.

There are two main series of fusion reactions that occur in the Sun:

- the **hydrogen cycle**, and
- the **carbon cycle**.

Each of the reactions in each cycle is a two-particle fusion reaction. This is because the simultaneous collision of more than two particles is too improbable to be significant.

The hydrogen (or proton–proton) cycle

Step 1

In the first fusion reaction of this series, two hydrogen-1 nuclei (protons) fuse to produce a hydrogen-2 (deuterium) nucleus. A helium-2 nucleus is *not* produced because a nucleus consisting only of two positively charged protons is *very* unstable.

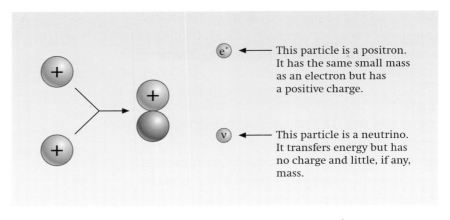

This particle is a positron. It has the same small mass as an electron but has a positive charge.

This particle is a neutrino. It transfers energy but has no charge and little, if any, mass.

$$^{1}_{1}\mathrm{H} + {}^{1}_{1}\mathrm{H} \rightarrow {}^{2}_{1}\mathrm{H} + {}^{0}_{1}\mathrm{e} + \nu$$

SAQ 3.3

Use the graph in *figure 1.9* on page 13 to estimate the energy transfer which results from the reaction in which two hydrogen nuclei fuse to form a deuterium nucleus.

Even inside the core of a star like the Sun, the reaction rate for the formation of deuterium is *very* slow (see *box 3B* on page 32). The Sun can only radiate energy at the rate it does because of its large volume and high density and hence the huge number of protons present (about 10^{56}). Because the formation of deuterium is by far the slowest step in the series of nuclear reactions that comprise the hydrogen cycle it is often referred to as the **deuterium bottleneck**.

Step 2

Once deuterium nuclei have been formed by the fusion of hydrogen nuclei, deuterium–deuterium fusion reactions could then occur.

There are so few deuterium nuclei present, however, that they are far more likely to fuse with another proton (hydrogen-1 nucleus):

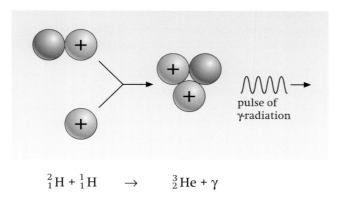

$$^2_1\text{H} + ^1_1\text{H} \quad \rightarrow \quad ^3_2\text{He} + \gamma$$

SAQ 3.4

Use the graph in *figure 1.9* to estimate the energy transfer which results from the fusion of a deuterium nucleus and a proton to form a helium–3 nucleus.

Step 3

Once helium-3 nuclei have formed, they are most likely to fuse with one of the very many hydrogen nuclei (protons) in the star. However, the product of such a fusion reaction – ^4Li – is so unstable that it splits back up again into a helium-3 nucleus and a proton almost as soon as it is formed. What happens, therefore, is that each helium-3 nucleus wanders around until it encounters another helium-3 nucleus when the following fusion reaction may occur:

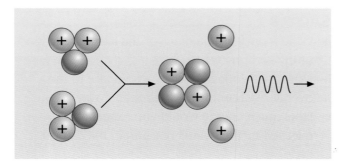

$$^3_2\text{He} + ^3_2\text{He} \quad \rightarrow \quad ^4_2\text{He} + 2^1_1\text{H} + \gamma$$

SAQ 3.5

Use the graph in *figure 1.9* to estimate the energy transfer which results from the fusion reaction between two helium–3 nuclei.

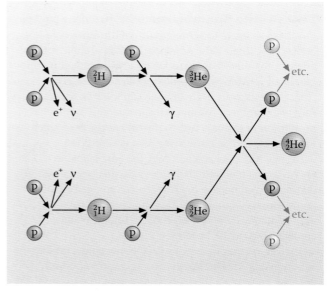

● **Figure 3.2** The hydrogen 'cycle', $4^1_1\text{H} \rightarrow ^4_2\text{He} + 2^0_1\text{e} + 2\nu$.

Figure 3.2 brings together the three fusion reactions described above in steps 1, 2 and 3.

SAQ 3.6

a Use the figures you have already calculated for the energy transfer at each step in the series of fusion reactions to find a value for the energy transferred by the overall reaction.

b Use your answer to **a** to calculate, for the overall series of hydrogen → helium fusion reactions:
  (i) the loss of rest mass (in u);
  (ii) the percentage loss of mass.

c Though the series of reactions is usually called the hydrogen *cycle*, this isn't really a correct description. Explain why.

Of the four electrons from the four hydrogen atoms, only two are needed to balance the charge on the resulting helium nucleus. The other two will meet up with the two positrons and all four particles will be annihilated.

Almost all of the neutrinos pass through the Sun's mass without interacting or transferring their energy in any way. This means that the energy they carry does not contribute to further nuclear reactions.

Box 3B The Sun as a nuclear fusion reactor

Physicists estimate the temperature of the Sun's core to be about 1.5×10^7 K. This corresponds to an *average* proton energy of about 1 keV, which is far less than the Coulomb barrier of 7.2 MeV. Some protons will, however, have sufficient energy to overcome the Coulomb barrier and fuse with another proton to form deuterium, but the proportion of protons with sufficient energy is so small that the rate of this nuclear reaction is very slow.

Despite this slow reaction rate, the Sun is able to radiate energy at the high rate that it does because of its high density and immense size. Each cubic centimetre of the Sun's core has a mass of 125 g and contains approximately 7.5×10^{25} protons. In total, the Sun contains around 10^{56} protons.

The very strong forces of gravitational attraction that act on matter in stars like the Sun are also important because they create the high temperature that makes it possible for nuclear fusion reactions to occur at all. In fact, unless a body has at least about one-tenth the mass of the Sun, its internal gravitational forces will not create a sufficiently high temperature to 'ignite' the first fusion reaction in the hydrogen cycle. So the body cannot become a star. The mass of Jupiter, the largest planet in the solar system, is about 100 times too small for it to have become a companion star to the Sun.

All that has been described in this chapter about nuclear fusion reactions in stars like the Sun has been worked out *theoretically* by physicists. You may well be wondering what *evidence* there is that the physicists' theories are correct. What is needed is some way of observing what is happening in the Sun's core.

Surprising as it may seem, there is, in fact, a way of making such observations. If the physicists are correct, for each four hydrogen nuclei that are converted into a helium nucleus via the reactions of the hydrogen cycle, two neutrinos (page 74) are produced. Once they have been created, these neutrinos travel with the speed of light but, unlike photons, hardly interact with matter at all. So they zip through the dense matter of the Sun and into space. Some of these neutrinos arrive at the Earth about 8 minutes later. This means that we can, in effect, look directly at the Sun's core.

The problem is that since neutrinos hardly interact at all with matter, it is extremely difficult to detect them. Physicists can, however, *just* manage to detect them using a tank containing nearly half a million litres of dry-cleaning fluid (C_2Cl_4, tetrachloroethene). This tank is shielded from other cosmic radiation by being placed 1 km below ground in a disused mine.

If the hydrogen cycle is occurring inside the Sun at the rate that physicists estimate, then about 10^{21} solar neutrinos should pass through the tank each day. Of these, just six would be expected to react with the fluid in the tank and convert a chlorine atom to a radioactive argon atom. These decay with a half-life of 35 days so that after 100 days an equilibrium should be obtained with around 60 radioactive argon atoms in the whole tank.

The results of this experiment indicate a rate of emission of solar neutrinos that is of the right *order*, although it is only at about one-third the predicted rate. This result is close enough to give support to physicists' theories, but the reason(s) for the discrepancy are still not known.

SAQ 3.7

The rate of reaction for proton–proton fusion at the Sun's core temperature is estimated to be 5×10^{-18} s^{-1} per proton. Estimate the rate at which these fusions occur in the Sun.

The carbon cycle

Though the Sun consists mainly of hydrogen and helium, about 1% of its mass comprises heavier elements. (The origin of these elements is described in *box 3C* on page 34.)

These heavier elements allow the fusion of hydrogen-1 into helium-4 to occur by alternative sequences of fusion reactions. The most important of the sequences is known as the carbon cycle and is shown in *figure 3.3*.

This sequence of reactions is genuinely a cycle. Overall, carbon-12 is neither created nor destroyed by the reaction sequence but passes through a series of intermediaries before finally being regenerated and entering the cycle again.

SAQ 3.8

a Write a nuclear equation for the *overall* reaction of the carbon cycle.

b How does your answer to **a** compare to the overall reaction for the hydrogen cycle?

c How much energy would you expect to be released by the overall reaction in the carbon cycle?

d The carbon cycle is sometimes called the CNO cycle. Explain why.

The carbon cycle does not have the 'deuterium bottleneck' which limits the overall rate of the hydrogen cycle but the fusion reactions in the carbon cycle have higher Coulomb barriers than

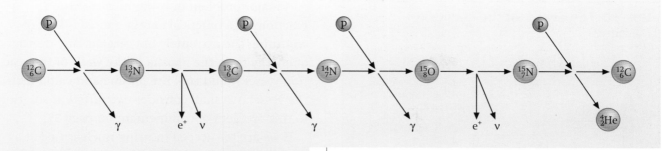

The series of reactions starts, and ends, with $^{12}_6$C. So it can be represented as a cycle.

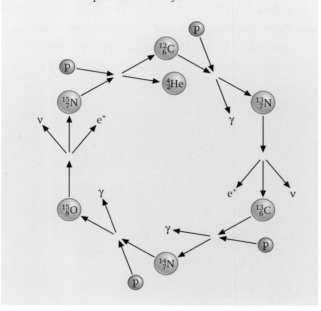

● **Figure 3.3** The carbon cycle.

in the hydrogen cycle. At the temperature of the Sun's core, the hydrogen cycle is the predominant series of fusion reactions. However, if the temperature were ten times as high, as it is in the core of some more massive stars, more hydrogen would be converted into helium via the carbon cycle.

Further fusion reactions in stars

Once a star has converted most of its hydrogen to helium (which physicists estimate will take the Sun a further 5×10^9 years) helium fusion begins:

$$3\,^4_2\text{He} \rightarrow \,^{12}_6\text{C}$$

SAQ 3.9

The above equation is for helium-4 → carbon-12 fusion *overall*. Explain why this reaction does not occur as a *single* fusion reaction.

The reactions involved in helium-4 → carbon-12 fusion have a higher Coulomb barrier, and so require a higher temperature than the hydrogen and carbon cycles. Further reactions involving the fusion of light nuclei, neutron capture and α-particle capture can then produce the nuclei of atoms as heavy as iron-56.

Producing more massive nuclei than iron-56 involves *endothermic* fusion reactions, i.e. reactions which require an overall *input* of energy. These reactions can only happen when huge amounts of energy are available, for example in the supernova explosions which are the final fate of stars which have sufficient mass (see *box 3C* on page 34).

SAQ 3.10

Use the binding energy graph in *figure 3.1* on page 29 to explain why nuclei heavier than iron–56 are not produced by normal nuclear fusion reactions in stars.

Achieving nuclear fusion on Earth

In order to produce controlled nuclear fusion reactions on Earth, from which useful amounts of energy would be available to generate electricity, we would need to:

■ heat the small nuclei used as fuel to temperatures of the order of 10^8 K, i.e. give the particles that are to fuse enough kinetic energy to overcome their mutual electrostatic repulsion;

■ maintain a sufficient density of small nuclei for a sufficient time to generate a comparable rate of energy release to that of a thermal fission reactor (about 1000 MW);

■ transfer this energy effectively for the production of steam to drive turbines.

Box 3C The origin of the chemical elements

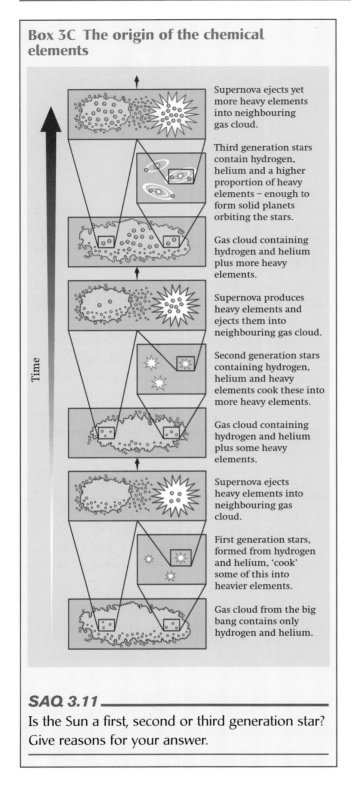

Time

Supernova ejects yet more heavy elements into neighbouring gas cloud.

Third generation stars contain hydrogen, helium and a higher proportion of heavy elements – enough to form solid planets orbiting the stars.

Gas cloud containing hydrogen and helium plus more heavy elements.

Supernova produces heavy elements and ejects them into neighbouring gas cloud.

Second generation stars containing hydrogen, helium and heavy elements cook these into more heavy elements.

Gas cloud containing hydrogen and helium plus some heavy elements.

Supernova ejects heavy elements into neighbouring gas cloud.

First generation stars, formed from hydrogen and helium, 'cook' some of this into heavier elements.

Gas cloud from the big bang contains only hydrogen and helium.

SAQ 3.11

Is the Sun a first, second or third generation star? Give reasons for your answer.

At the very high temperatures that are required for fusion reactions to occur, atoms are stripped of their electrons. In a fusion reactor, therefore, there would be an electrically neutral mixture of atomic nuclei (positively charged ions) and electrons. Such a mixture is known as **plasma**.

A major problem in using nuclear fusion reactions as a practical energy source is that of **confining** the extremely hot plasma. Any transfer of energy from the plasma to the walls of the reaction vessel would cool the plasma and could melt the vessel. We shall consider two different solutions to this problem of confinement on page 35.

If we are to succeed in using nuclear fusion as an energy source, it is also important to select the most appropriate fusion reaction. This needs to be a **single-stage reaction**, rather than the multi-stage reactions that occur in the Sun. The most promising candidate is the fusion reaction between hydrogen-2 (deuterium) and hydrogen-3 (tritium).

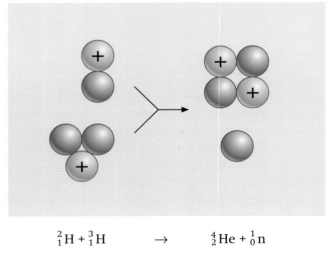

$$^{2}_{1}H + ^{3}_{1}H \rightarrow ^{4}_{2}He + ^{1}_{0}n$$

There are three main reasons for preferring this D–T (deuterium–tritium) fusion reaction:

1 the Coulomb barrier for D–T fusion is about the same as for D–D fusion;
2 the energy released by D–T fusion is much greater than for D–D fusion;
3 the D–T fusion reaction produces a net energy output at a lower temperature than the D–D fusion reaction.

For nuclei other than the isotopes of hydrogen, the Coulomb barriers are even higher and the temperatures required for fusion reactions are completely unattainable.

SAQ 3.12

Use the binding energy graph in *figure 1.9* on page 13 to estimate the energy released during D–T fusion.

SAQ 3.13

D–D fusion can produce either helium-3 nuclei or hydrogen-3 nuclei.

a Write nuclear equations for each of these fusion reactions.

b Use the binding energy graph in *figure 1.9* to estimate the energy released by each fusion reaction.

c Suggest why hydrogen-1 (H–H) fusion is not an appropriate one to use in a terrestrial fusion reactor.

There is, however, a problem with both the D–D and the D–T fusion reactions: 80% of the energy released is carried as the kinetic energy of neutrons. Neutrons have no electrical charge which means that they do not transfer their energy readily to coolant atoms via collisions but penetrate to the nuclei of atoms where they can then cause nuclear reactions. This makes it difficult to extract energy and transfer it to a steam generator. In a thermal fission reactor, on the other hand, the released energy is carried mainly as the kinetic energy of the fission fragments, which transfer this energy very readily to the coolant.

To transfer energy from the energetic neutrons produced in the fusion reaction, these neutrons are first captured by the nuclei in a blanket of liquid lithium surrounding the reaction vessel. The following nuclear reactions occur:

$$^6_3\text{Li} + ^1_0\text{n} \rightarrow ^4_2\text{He} + ^3_1\text{H}$$

$$^7_3\text{Li} + ^1_0\text{n} \rightarrow ^4_2\text{He} + ^3_1\text{H} + ^1_0\text{n}$$

As a result of these nuclear reactions, the energy of the neutrons is transferred to the helium-4 and hydrogen-3 atoms that are produced. These then transfer the energy, via collisions, to the molten lithium. Finally, the energy from the hot molten lithium could be used to produce steam for driving turbines.

SAQ 3.14

The hydrogen-3 has to be extracted from the lithium blanket. What do you think is then done with it?

The other 20% of the energy released during D–T fusion is realised as the kinetic energy of the

α-particles (helium nuclei) produced by the fusion reaction. These high energy α-particles collide with other ions and so maintain the plasma's high temperature. When the power from these α-particles is sufficient to maintain the plasma temperature, the reaction becomes self-heating, a condition known as **ignition**.

How plasma is confined

There are two approaches to solving the problem of plasma confinement:

- **magnetic**, via carefully designed magnetic fields;
- **inertial**, in which the material to be fused is very suddenly heated and compressed.

A third method of confinement using **gravitational** forces is only possible in very massive bodies such as the Sun whose whole core is a gigantic fusion reactor.

Magnetic confinement

Plasma can be confined by means of a carefully designed magnetic field (*figure 3.4*), sometimes called a 'magnetic bottle'.

Because the plasma contains ions, it is conducting. It is contained inside a toroidal (doughnut-shaped) vacuum vessel which encircles one limb of a transformer. It thus acts as the single turn secondary coil of the transformer. The primary coil of many turns is wound onto another limb of

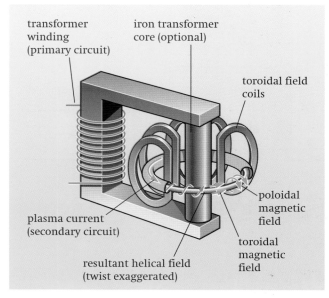

Figure 3.4 Magnetic confinement of plasma.

the magnetic core. When an alternating primary current is passed through this coil it induces a current of several million amperes in the plasma.

SAQ 3.15

Using the theory of the transformer, explain how it is possible to obtain such high currents in the plasma.

The toroidal field coils which surround the toroidal vacuum vessel provide a circular magnetic field, called the **toroidal** field along the path of the plasma ring. In addition, the plasma current creates its own magnetic field around itself (the **poloidal** field). These two magnetic fields have a resultant which is helical.

A moving charge normally follows a helical path along a magnetic field line. The sketch of *figure 3.5* shows the path of a positive ion in relation to a straight magnetic field line. Inside the vacuum vessel the path of the ions is therefore quite complicated – a spiral on a spiral! However, the important fact is that the ions are *captive* within the magnetic field and so cannot touch the walls.

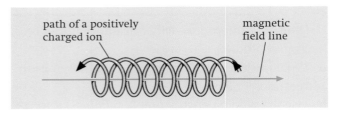

Figure 3.5 A positive ion spiralling round a straight magnetic field line.

The plasma has electrical resistance, so the huge plasma current results in the transfer of thermal energy to the plasma, which raises its temperature. As its temperature rises, however, the resistance of the plasma decreases and the ohmic heating effect diminishes. Hence, to achieve the temperatures required ($10^8 - 10^9$ K, i.e. particle energies of 10 – 100 keV), additional methods of heating must be used.

This can be done by using radio-frequency waves which induce toroidal currents in the plasma.

Alternatively, deuterium ions can be accelerated to high energies outside the reaction vessel and then injected into the plasma.

Energy has to be supplied at a rate of tens of megawatts to ignite the plasma.

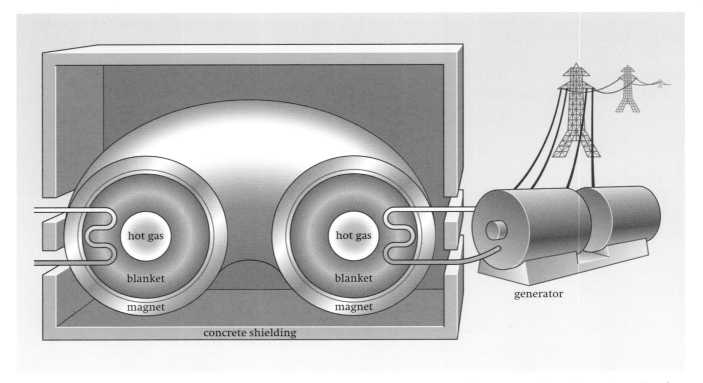

● **Figure 3.6** A blanket of liquid lithium captures neutrons from the fusion reaction. Tritium is produced as fast as it is used up in the fusion reaction. The kinetic energy from the captured neutrons heats up the lithium. This thermal energy is then transferred to steam which is used to drive turbines and generate electricity.

The experimental Joint European Torus (JET) at Culham in Oxfordshire uses magnetic confinement (see *figure 3.5*).

Inertial confinement

In this method of confinement, a tiny pellet containing deuterium and tritium is bombarded from all sides by a brief but intense laser pulse. This heats and compresses the pellet so quickly that a high enough temperature and density for fusion to occur is produced before the pellet has time to blow apart.

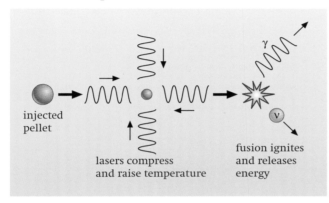

injected pellet

lasers compress and raise temperature

fusion ignites and releases energy

Pellets are injected into the reaction vessel, compressed and ignited 10–100 times per second. The laser pulses require huge amounts of power, albeit for very brief periods, so this approach is not likely to prove practicable unless and until much more efficient lasers are developed.

Prospects for nuclear fusion as an energy source

Nuclear fusion offers what is potentially an environmentally friendly and sustainable energy source:

- As with nucleur fission, but unlike when fossil fuels are burned, there is no emission of greenhouse gases or of the gases that produce acid rain.
- The small nuclei that are used as the nuclear fuel are plentiful and easy to obtain. For example:
  - About 0.015% of naturally occurring hydrogen atoms, e.g. in water, are hydrogen-2. Furthermore, because of the large mass difference between hydrogen-1 and hydrogen-2, they are relatively easy to separate by physical methods.
  - Hydrogen-3 can be made by bombarding hydrogen-2 or lithium-3 with neutrons (the latter reaction occurring in the energy-capturing lithium blanket surrounding the fusion reaction vessel).
- Neither the products of the fusion process, nor the reactor itself once its useful life is over, present problems with radioactive substances having long half-lives. The radioactive tritium produced in the lithium has a short half-life and is in any case itself used as a fuel in the reactor.
- Providing the materials out of which the reactor is made are carefully selected, the reactor itself will not present problems with radioactive materials having a long half-life once its useful life is over.
- Fusion will be an inherently safe system with the amount of fuel in use at any given time being sufficient for only a few seconds of operation; any form of malfunction will stop the reaction very quickly (within about 1 minute).

There are, however, many serious technological problems to be solved if the potential of nuclear fusion as an energy source is ever to be realised in practice.

Difficulties Encountered in the JET Project

These are considerable and many, but among the most severe are:

- Achieving a magnetic field which contains the plasma for a long enough period to allow fusion to work. For ignition to be achieved, the fusion product [temperature × confinement time × plasma density] has to exceed a critical value. When very high temperature plasma touches the walls it causes evaporation which leads to contamination of the plasma. It also erodes the wall and shortens the life of the reactor.
- Removing from the plasma the by-products (mainly helium) and other impurities.
- In the longer term, it is intended that JET should be succeeded by a larger prototype reactor. One of the major challenges will be to progress from a *pulsed* reaction to one which operates continuously.

SUMMARY

◆ The merging of small atomic nuclei to form larger atomic nuclei is called nuclear fusion.

◆ Nuclear fusion can occur because the resulting nuclei have less binding energy per nucleon than the nuclei which fused to produce them and so are more stable. This means that nuclear fusion results in the release of energy and a corresponding loss of mass.

◆ Before two hydrogen nuclei (protons) can fuse, work must be done to overcome the electrostatic (Coulomb) force of repulsion between them. The work that is done increases the electric potential energy of the protons. For this to happen, the protons must have sufficient kinetic energy to overcome the Coulomb barrier and become sufficiently close to each other for the strong force to act between them.

◆ If you are told how much work needs to be done (i.e. the size of the coulomb or electrical potential energy barrier) for fusion to occur, you can calculate the temperature required for this to happen using the relationship:

$$E_k = \frac{3}{2} kT$$

where E_k is kinetic energy (in joules), T is the temperature (in kelvin) and k is the Boltzmann constant, $1.38 \times 10^{-23} \, \text{J K}^{-1}$.

◆ In stars such as the Sun, two series of fusion reactions occur. These are known as the carbon cycle and the hydrogen cycle. [You must be able, when given appropriate details of the reactions in the hydrogen and carbon cycles:
   – to explain what is happening;
   – to construct and interpret nuclear equations for the fusion reactions.
You must also be able to estimate, from a graph of how binding energy per nucleon varies with the number of nucleons in a nucleus, the energy available from fusion reactions such as hydrogen → helium.]

◆ The Sun is a nuclear fusion reactor, its great mass producing a large gravitational force which has resulted in its core being raised to a sufficiently high temperature for hydrogen → helium fusion to occur. Although the reaction is at a very low rate per proton, the Sun contains so many protons that the overall rate of reaction and of energy production is quite high.

◆ Scientists and technologists are working on the development of nuclear fusion as an energy source on Earth. The small nuclei used as fuel need to be at a very high temperature (at least $10^8 \, \text{K}$). At such high temperatures, there is an electrically neutral mixture of positively charged atomic nuclei (ions) and electrons known as plasma.

◆ A major problem with making a nuclear fusion reaction is that of confining the extremely hot plasma so that it retains its energy and does not melt (or vaporise) the materials from which the reactors are made. In the Sun, gravitational forces confine the plasma. On Earth plasma is confined using strong magnetic fields or by heating and compressing the fuel very quickly (inertial confinement).

◆ The most favoured reaction for a practical fusion reactor is the D–T (deuterium–tritium) fusion reaction. This is because it is a single-stage fusion reaction, and compared to other single-stage reactions:
   – it has a relatively low Coulomb barrier;
   – it releases more energy per fusion;
   – it gives a net energy gain, taking into account radiation energy losses, at a lower temperature.

◆ The prototype Joint European Torus (JET) fusion reactor uses D–T fusion and magnetic confinement.

◆ The energy released in nuclear fusion reactions is mainly carried by fast-moving neutrons. These are captured in a blanket of liquid lithium surrounding the reactor. Their energy is mainly transferred to the products of these nuclear reactions as thermal energy. This can then be used to generate steam as in other power stations.

◆ If nuclear fusion reactors could be successfully developed on a commercial scale they would have two great advantages: they would have a virtually unlimited supply of fuel and they cause hardly any pollution.

Questions

1 a Heavier nuclei can more easily be made by neutron capture than by nuclear fusion. Explain why.
   b Why are there limits to how much larger a nucleus can be made by neutron capture?

2 Use the data from the table to calculate the loss in mass (in u) and hence the energy released (in MeV):
   a for each stage in the carbon cycle;
   b for the whole cycle.
      (1u = 931.5 MeV)

3 The rest mass of a positron is 0.0005 u. Compare and contrast nuclear fission and nuclear fusion as energy sources.

Nucleus	Mass (u)
^{1}H	1.0078
^{4}He	4.0026
^{12}C	12.0000
^{13}N	13.0057
^{13}C	13.0034
^{14}N	14.0031
^{15}O	15.0031
^{15}N	15.0001

CHAPTER 4

The search for fundamental particles

By the end of this chapter you should be able to:

1 explain what is meant by a fundamental particle;

2 appreciate that the discovery of antimatter meant that scientists had to extend their simple model of everything being made from protons, neutrons and electrons;

3 recall that the positron is the antiparticle of the electron;

4 recall that particle–antiparticle pairs annihilate one another to produce high-energy (γ-ray) photons;

5 recall that particles which are affected by the strong force (interaction) are called hadrons;

6 recall that protons and neutrons are just two of many different types of hadron;

7 recall that all hadrons are thought to be unstable to some degree and hence decay;

8 recall that protons are relatively stable;

9 recall that neutrons within a nucleus are relatively stable but that free neutrons are unstable, with a half-life of about 15 minutes, and decay to produce a proton and a β-particle (electron).

The idea of fundamental particles

There are billions of different things that exist in or that happen in the world around us. There are billions more things that people can create or that they can cause to happen. Scientists look for **patterns** in all these things so that they can make better sense of them. They also try to explain the many things that exist or that can happen by telling **explanatory stories** in terms of just a few key ideas. The idea that everything is made of a small number of **fundamental particles** – particles which are not themselves made of anything smaller – is one of these key scientific ideas.

Atoms

This idea that everything is made of particles goes back to the Ancient Greeks 2500 years ago (*atomos* is the Greek word for 'can't be cut'). The idea was re-introduced into modern science at the beginning of the nineteenth century by John Dalton (*box 4A*). Dalton's idea that all the millions of different substances in the world are made up from the atoms of a small number of different elements joined together in different ways is the foundation of the modern science of chemistry. In 1869, Dmitri Mendeleev made another important step forward in scientific understanding. He discovered that when elements were listed in order of the masses of their atoms, they could then be arranged in a pattern called the periodic table such that elements in the same column

(Group) had similar properties. This pattern
enabled Mendeleev to predict the existence of
previously unknown elements, which scientists
then looked for and eventually discovered.

Altogether, there are 92 naturally occurring
elements. Before scientists had actually found all
of these elements, however, they had already
discovered that the atoms of these elements were
not, as they had hoped, the truly fundamental
particles from which everything else is made.

SAQ 4.1

Explain why the word *atom* is a very appropriate
term for a fundamental particle.

Box 4C The structure of an atom

This diagram of a lithium atom, $^{7}_{3}\text{Li}$, is *not* to scale.

nucleus { proton ——
neutron ——

3 electrons in this region ——

Diameters of atoms are of the order 10^{-10} m. Diameters
of atomic nuclei are of the order of 10^{-14} m.

SAQ 4.2

About how many times smaller are the nuclei of
atoms than atoms themselves?

Protons, neutrons and electrons

During the last few years of the nineteenth century
and the early part of the twentieth century, scientists discovered that atoms were themselves made
of smaller, more fundamental particles. The electron, for example, was discovered by J. J. Thomson
in 1897 and experiments carried out in 1909–1911
for Ernest Rutherford by his colleagues Hans Geiger
and Ernest Marsden showed that atoms had a
small, dense, positively charged nucleus (box 4B).
By the early 1930s, scientists had established the
basic structure of atoms (*box 4C*): each atom has a
nucleus made up of particles called **protons** and
neutrons and this nucleus is surrounded by
electrons in different energy levels or shells.

The arrangement of electrons in the various
energy levels not only explained the pattern of
elements in the periodic table but also explained
why atoms of different elements react with each
other in the ways that they do. What appeared to
be three fundamental particles – the proton (p),
the neutron (n) and the electron (e⁻) – and the way
that these particles were arranged in atoms
enabled scientists to understand millions of different chemical substances and chemical reactions.

This very powerful explanatory story in terms
of just three fundamental particles was matched
by a parallel story involving three fundamental
forces, in terms of which all other forces could be
understood.

Box 4D Three fundamental forces

Gravitational force

- Acts between all masses
- Is always a force of attraction
- Is 10^{36} times weaker than electromagnetic force
- Acts at any distance but proportional to $1/[\text{distance}]^2$
- Is not important for subatomic particles

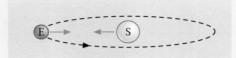

The gravitational force is important for large masses. It holds the Earth in orbit around the Sun and holds you on the Earth.

Electromagnetic force

- Acts between charged bodies
- Can attract or repel
- Acts at any distance but is proportional to $1/[\text{distance}]^2$
- Attractions and repulsions normally cancel for bodies bigger than molecules

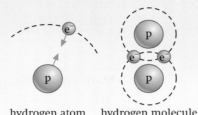

hydrogen atom   hydrogen molecule

Electromagnetic forces hold electrons to nuclei in atoms, hold atoms together in compounds and hold together solid and liquid substances.

Strong force

- Acts between nucleons (protons and neutrons)
- Is normally a force of attraction but becomes repulsive when nucleons are very close
- Is around 100 times stronger than the electromagnetic force
- Only acts over distances less than 10^{-14} m

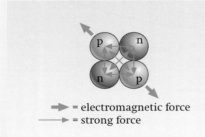

➡ = electromagnetic force
→ = strong force

The strong force holds nucleons together in the nuclei of atoms.

SAQ 4.3

a About how many times stronger than the gravitational force is the strong force?

b Explain why the strong force is very effective at holding the nuclei of atoms together but plays no part in holding electrons to nuclei or atoms to each other.

The three fundamental forces (see *box 4D*) are:
- a **gravitational** force of attraction between all masses;
- electrical and magnetic forces which are different aspects of the same **electromagnetic** force (for charged particles which are more or less stationary this is mainly an *electrostatic* force);

- a third force which acts between nucleons (protons and neutrons) but only when these are very close together and which does not act at all on electrons. This force holds together the nucleus of each atom and so has to be a **strong** force in order to overcome the electrical forces which cause positively charged protons to repel each other.

Being able to explain so many things in terms of just three fundamental particles and three fundamental forces was a very satisfactory state of affairs. Unfortunately, it was not to last for very long.

Particles galore

By the early 1930s, just as the powerful explanatory story in terms of protons, neutrons and electrons was becoming firmly established, scientists were beginning to realise that things were not, in fact, quite as simple and straightforward as they had hoped.

Antimatter

One problem for the idea that there are just three kinds of fundamental particle – protons, neutrons and electrons – came from the discovery of **antimatter**.

The idea that antimatter might exist arose when physicists were working with two radical new theories that Albert Einstein had proposed as early as 1905:

Box 4E Photoelectric effect

When light, or higher frequency forms of electromagnetic radiation, fall on to certain metals, electrons may be emitted from the metal. This is called the photoelectric effect.

If the photoelectric effect happens at all with a particular metal and a particular frequency of radiation, then it continues to happen even when the radiation has a very low intensity. Fewer electrons are emitted, but the electrons that are emitted have exactly the same kinetic energy as when the radiation is more intense.

These observations can readily be explained if electromagnetic radiation of a particular frequency travels as equal sized packets of energy (quanta) in the form of massless particles called photons. The theory of how these quanta behave is called quantum theory (see *Physics 1*, chapter 16, especially pages 138–40).

[You will meet the related idea that particles of matter can behave as waves in chapter 7.]

Albert Einstein.

- To explain the photoelectric effect he suggested that light, and other types of electro-magnetic waves, travelled as tiny packets (or quanta) of energy which could be regarded as massless particles called photons (see *box 4E* for further details of this idea).
- His special theory of relativity showed that mass and energy were not, as had previously been thought, completely separate quantities but were really different aspects of one and the same thing. In other words what we normally think of as mass has an energy equivalent and vice versa.

Einstein had shown that electromagnetic waves travel in the form of particles called photons. In 1925, the French physicist Louis de Broglie showed that Einstein's theories also required moving particles of matter to behave like waves. In 1928, when Paul Dirac was working out in detail how this idea applied to electrons, he was surprised to find that his equations meant that another type of particle must exist with the same mass as an electron but with the opposite electrical charge, i.e. positive (+) rather than negative (−). Dirac tried to get rid of this unwelcome idea from his

equations but was unable to do so. Antielectrons or **positrons** (e⁺) had to exist if Dirac's theory was to work.

[Note: Another way of representing an antiparticle is to use the symbol for the corresponding particle with a bar above it meaning 'anti'. When this way of representing particles is used, any electrical charges on particles are *not* shown, because this would be very confusing. So:
- an electron can be represented as e⁻ or e;
- an antielectron can be represented as e⁺ or ē.
Sometimes one of these ways of representing particles is more appropriate than the other. At other times either can be used.]

In 1932, Carl Anderson, who did not at the time know about Dirac's theory, detected positrons in cosmic radiation, high-energy particles that enter the Earth's atmosphere from space (see *figure 5.2* on page 50). Ironically, definite experimental evidence for the existence of the neutron was also first obtained in 1932, so that as soon as the idea that there were just three types of fundamental particle – electrons, protons and neutrons – was properly established it was already being undermined!

Physicists then found that combining the quantum theory of energy with the special theory of relativity required that there must also be a type of antimatter particle corresponding to each type of fundamental particle. Since there are protons (p or p⁺), for example, there must also be antiprotons (p̄ or p⁻) with the same mass as protons but with the opposite electrical charge; and since there are neutrons (n or n⁰) there must also be antineutrons (n̄ or n̄⁰).

Antimatter particles are, however, difficult to find because whenever they appear in our world of matter, they very quickly meet up with their equivalent matter particle. The matter particle and antimatter particle then annihilate each other (*figure 4.1*) to produce packets (quanta) of energy in the form of high-energy photons or, in other words, bursts of γ-radiation (gamma radiation).

SAQ 4.4

In science fiction stories, antimatter is sometimes used to make antigravity devices. Explain what is wrong with this idea.

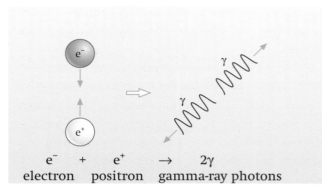

$$e^- + e^+ \rightarrow 2\gamma$$
electron positron gamma-ray photons

● **Figure 4.1** Annihilation of matter and antimatter releases energy.

SAQ 4.5

It is easy to understand the idea of antielectrons and antiprotons (particles with the same mass as electrons and protons, respectively, but with the opposite electrical charge). Why is the idea of an antineutron more puzzling? [The way that this puzzle is resolved is explained on page 68.]

The discovery of more types of matter particles

Evidence for there being more types of fundamental particle than protons, neutrons and electrons (plus their antiparticles) also came from cosmic radiation. In 1937 Anderson and a colleague discovered a 'heavy' electron, a particle with a negative electrical charge but with a mass more than 200 times greater than that of an electron. This particle is called a **muon** (μ^-). In 1947 particles called **pions** (π^+ and π^-) were also discovered in cosmic rays by Cecil Powell.

Box 4F Two families of particles

As physicists discovered more particles and studied their properties, they realised that the particles belonged to two different groups:

■ some particles, including protons, neutrons and pions, are affected by the strong force;

■ other particles, including electrons and muons, are not affected by the strong force.

Particles which are affected by the strong force are called **hadrons**.

Particles which are not affected by the strong force are called **leptons**.

[Note: The strong force is sometimes referred to as the strong **interaction**.]

Box 4G Producing pions in a particle accelerator

When two protons collide with sufficient energy you can end up with a proton, a neutron and a positive pion.

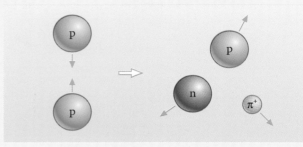

You can write down this interaction as a word equation:

proton + proton → proton + neutron + positive pion

You can also write it down as a symbol equation:

$$p^+ + p^+ \rightarrow p^+ + n^0 + \pi^+ \text{ [pi-plus]}$$

[Later, when we examine in detail what happens to electrical charges during particle reactions, it will be helpful to use the symbols p^+ for a proton and n^0 for a neutron. So it is useful to get into the habit of using them as soon as possible.]

SAQ 4.6

When a proton and a neutron collide, two protons and a negative pion (pi-minus particle) may be produced.

Write down this interaction:

a as a word equation;

b as a symbol equation.

During the late 1940s and early 1950s, several more hadrons (see *box 4F*) were discovered in cosmic radiation including:

K (kappa), Λ (lambda) and Σ (sigma).

[All of these symbols are letters of the Greek alphabet, like the letter π (pi). Because K is in our alphabet, this hadron is often called kay.] Scientists had, by this time, become dissatisfied with just waiting for new particles to arrive at their detectors from space. They developed machines with which they could produce new particles by accelerating charged particles such as protons to very high speeds and making them collide with other particles (*box 4G*). These machines are called **particle accelerators**. (You can read about how these machines work in chapter 6.) In 1948, pions were produced in a particle accelerator called a **cyclotron**.

As particle accelerators that were capable of producing beams of particles with higher and higher energies were developed, more and more different types of hadron were discovered.

Why there are only two types of hadron in ordinary matter

Many different types of hadron exist, but we find only two types of hadron – protons and neutrons – in ordinary matter. The reason for this is that most hadrons are very unstable and exist only for the tiniest fraction of a second (usually in the range 10^{-10} to 10^{-23} s). They then decay into different particles, for example:

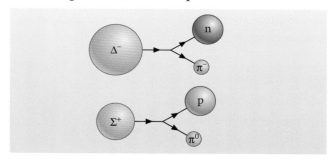

SAQ 4.7
Describe, using symbol equations, what happens when the following hadrons decay:

a a Δ^--particle;

b a Σ^+-particle.

It is important to be clear about what is happening when hadrons decay. A Δ^--particle, for example, is not made up of a neutron and a negative pion, so it isn't correct to say that it splits up into these two particles. What happens is that the Δ^--particle changes into a neutron and a

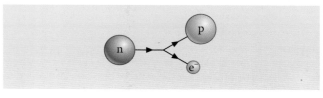

$$n^0 \quad \rightarrow \quad p^+ + e^- \quad [\beta\text{-particle}]$$

negative pion. The Δ^--particle ceases to exist and two different particles exist in its place.

The only stable hadrons are protons and even they may not be completely stable (see chapter 8).

Neutrons are only stable when they are inside a stable atomic nucleus. Free neutrons decay with a half-life of about 15 minutes. In other words, every 15 minutes about half of any sample of free neutrons will decay and, during any 15-minute period, there is a 50% chance that any particular neutron will decay.

[Note: The above equation for neutron decay is not quite complete. Neutron decay, β-radiation and proton decay are all considered in more detail in chapter 8.]

When an unstable nucleus emits a β-particle, this is caused by a neutron in the nucleus decaying in exactly the same way as a free neutron decays.

SAQ 4.8
A K-zero particle can decay into two pions, one of them positive and the other negative. Write a symbol equation for this decay.

'Who ordered that?'

By the early 1960s, particle physicists had discovered well over a hundred different types of hadron (*box 4H*). If you are dismayed by this, and are increasingly concerned about how the neat and tidy story of protons, neutrons and electrons has become a lot more complicated and confusing, you are in very good company. Many scientists were also, quite understandably, dismayed by the outcome of their investigations. Instead of a simple yet powerful story that they could tell in terms of just three fundamental particles, they now had a whole 'zoo' of different particles and new particles were still being discovered. Enrico Fermi said that if he had known that physics would turn like that, he would have studied zoology instead. Many physicists sympathised with the feelings of Isodor Rabi, who greeted the discovery of the muon with the comment 'Who ordered that?'

Box 4H By early 1960s: well over 100 fundamental particles?

The discovery of antimatter and of many other types of particle besides protons, neutrons and electrons destroyed the simple yet powerful idea that there are just three types of fundamental particle.

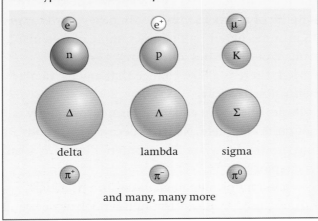

delta   lambda   sigma

and many, many more

During the period 1964–1970, physicists did, in fact, manage to discover patterns in the types of particles and in what happened when different particles collided or decayed. They were also able to explain these patterns in terms of a relatively small number of truly fundamental particles. The new ideas which scientists developed are described in chapters 7 and 8 of this book.

Before looking at how physicists actually resolved the problem of fundamental particles, however, we shall first consider three other questions which may already have occurred to you:

- How can high-energy collisions between particles actually produce additional particles which didn't previously exist?
- How do physicists detect incredibly tiny subatomic particles which often exist only for an incredibly short period of time?
- How can we tell what type of particles have been detected?

These questions are considered in chapter 5.

Chapter 6 then describes the different kinds of accelerators used in particle physics and explains how they work.

SUMMARY

- For every type of subatomic particle there is a matching antimatter particle which has the same mass but the opposite electrical charge.

- The antiparticle of the electron (e⁻) is called the positron (e⁺).

- There is a strong force (interaction) between nucleons (protons and neutrons). This force holds them together in the nuclei of atoms.

- There are many other particles besides protons and neutrons which are affected by the strong force. All of these particles are called hadrons.

- Most hadrons are very unstable and quickly decay into different particles.

- Neutrons that are inside a stable nucleus are themselves stable, but free neutrons are unstable. They have a half-life of about 15 minutes and decay to produce a proton and a β-particle (electron).*

- Protons are the only very stable hadrons but even they may not be completely stable.*

- Electrons belong to a group of particles call leptons which are not affected by the strong force.

[* The summary to chapter 8 contains additions to these statements.]

Questions

1 Briefly outline how scientists' ideas about which particles are fundamental changed from the beginning of the nineteenth century until the early 1960s.

2 Suppose that many other particles were stable in addition to electrons, protons and the neutrons in atomic nuclei. What difference do you think that this would make to the world?

Creating and detecting particles

How particles can appear from nowhere

Imagine that you are playing a game of pool. You use a cue to make the white ball move. This ball then travels along the table and strikes a red ball. As a result of the collision, the two balls then move off in different directions from the point of the collision. This is exactly what you would expect to happen. But then you notice that something else has also happened: a small glass marble has appeared from nowhere and is moving off from the point of the collision in a third direction!

If this were to happen you would, quite rightly, not believe your eyes. But it is exactly the kind of thing that does often happen when subatomic particles collide.

The diagram shows what can happen when a fast-moving proton collides with a stationary proton:

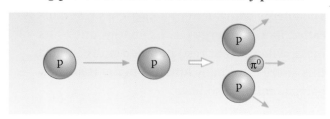

A neutral pion (π^0), also called pi-zero, seems to have appeared from nowhere.

To solve this puzzle we must once again use Einstein's idea that mass and energy are related by the equation:

$$E = mc^2$$

In nuclear fission and fusion reactions, for example, mass is converted into energy. In particle collisions, the opposite can occur: energy can be converted into mass. In the collision shown above, the total kinetic energy of the particles after the collision is less than the kinetic energy of the fast-moving proton before the collision. The 'lost' energy has created the mass of the pi-zero particle.

A pion can, of course, be created by the collision only if the proton has enough kinetic energy in the first place. That's why it has to be a fast-moving proton. If the proton doesn't have enough kinetic energy to create the pion, the colliding protons will just bounce off each other in the same way that colliding pool balls do:

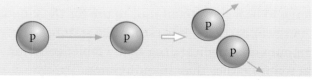

or, if the protons collide square-on:

SAQ 5.1

Calculate the kinetic energy (in joules, J) needed to create a π^0 particle. (Speed of light, $c = 3 \times 10^8\,\mathrm{m\,s^{-1}}$.)

Particle	Mass (kg $\times 10^{-27}$)
proton	1.673
neutron	1.675
π^0	0.241
π^-	0.250

SAQ 5.2

The following equation shows what can happen when a fast-moving proton collides with a neutron:

$$p^+ + n^0 \rightarrow p^+ + p^+ + \pi^-$$

Calculate the kinetic energy (in joules, J) that is lost in this collision.

Choosing appropriate units for the energy and mass of particles

Whenever we make measurements, it is most convenient to use units that are an appropriate size for whatever we are measuring. Window frames, for example, are made accurate to the nearest millimetre so it is convenient to quote their size in millimetres. For a car or plane journey between two cities, however, we only need to know the distance to within a few kilometres, so this is the most appropriate unit to use.

As you will have found when doing SAQs 5.1 and 5.2, joules and kilograms are not very appropriate units to use for the kinetic energy and the mass of subatomic particles.

Kinetic energy

The standard unit of energy – the joule – is far too large to be a convenient unit to use for the kinetic energy of particles. It is rather like stating the amount of a medical drug that a tablet contains in tonnes rather than in milligrams.

A more suitable unit of energy is related to what physicists actually do with particles in their experiments. To give electrically charged particles a lot of kinetic energy for their experiments, physicists accelerate them using electrical fields. Charged subatomic particles all have the same size of charge as an electron (though it may be positive rather than negative). So a unit that we could use for the kinetic energy of a particle is the energy that is transferred to an electron when it is accelerated through a potential difference of one volt. This unit of energy is called the **electron-volt (eV)**.

As a matter of fact, the electron-volt turns out to be rather too small a unit for convenience, so particle physicists usually use:

- the **mega-electron-volt (MeV)** = 10^6 eV

or

- the **giga-electron-volt (GeV)** = 10^9 eV

SAQ 5.3

Use the following information to calculate the number of joules in 1 eV. The amount of energy, in joules, that is transferred when a charge Q coulombs moves across a potential difference of V volts is given by:

$$E = QV$$

The charge on an electron is 1.602×10^{-19} C.

Mass

The standard unit of mass – the kilogram – is also far too large a unit to be convenient for subatomic particles. The mass of a proton or a neutron, for example, is of the order of 10^{-27} kg and electrons have a mass almost 2000 times smaller still.

In fact, when dealing with subatomic particles, it is best not to use ordinary units of mass at all. In particle physics, we are often concerned with the conversion of energy into mass or vice versa. It is usually most convenient, therefore, to consider the mass of a particle in terms of its energy equivalent using the relationship:

$$m = E/c^2$$

The energy equivalent of a particle's rest mass is called its **rest energy** (i.e. its energy, due to its mass, when it is at rest) in order to distinguish this energy from any kinetic energy that the particle might also have:

E	=	E_0	+	E_k
overall energy of particle	=	rest energy (rest mass)	+	kinetic energy

The total overall energy of the particles involved in a collision or decay is always the same after the interaction as it was before. Energy – when rest energy is also taken into account – is *conserved*.

The rest energy of a proton is 0.938 GeV, i.e. nearly 1 GeV. This is very convenient since the mass of a proton is 1.007 u, which is very close to 1 u (1 atomic mass unit). This means that:

$$1\,u \approx 1\,GeV$$

SAQ 5.4

The mass of a neutron is 1.675×10^{-27} kg. Calculate the rest energy of a neutron in GeV.

SAQ 5.5

Use information from the table below to state how much energy a fast-moving proton must lose, during a collision with a stationary proton, to create a negative pion.

Particle	Rest energy (GeV)
π^+, π^-	0.134
π^0	0.135
e^+, e^-	5.11×10^{-4}
Δ (all types)	1.232

SAQ 5.6

a What is the rest energy of an electron in MeV?
b Calculate the minimum energy of the γ-ray photons produced when an electron and a positron annihilate each other:

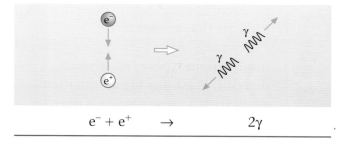

$$e^- + e^+ \quad \rightarrow \quad 2\gamma$$

Obtaining particle traces

When physicists are doing experiments with subatomic particles, these particles are obviously much too small to see. So physicists need some other way of detecting where these particles are and what is happening to them.

There's one type of particle detector that you've seen in action thousands of times – an ordinary TV screen. When fast-moving electrons hit the chemical substances (phosphors) on the inside of the screen, tiny glints (scintillations) of light are emitted. The picture is made up from thousands of these scintillations. The fact that atoms have a small dense nucleus was first discovered in 1911 by firing a stream of charged particles at the atoms in some gold leaf and observing where these particles then went by observing the scintillations that they produced. A similar method was used in 1968 to find out about the internal structure of hadrons (see chapter 7).

In most particle physics experiments, however, scientists are looking for evidence of particular, often quite rare, events in which various individual particles are created and/or decay. These particles are usually moving very rapidly and often exist only for a very short period of time, so scientists need some way of obtaining traces of the paths along which the particles move during their brief existence.

SAQ 5.7

A particle created during a collision moves at one-third the speed of light and exists for 10^{-9} seconds before decaying. How far will the particle travel during its existence?

● **Figure 5.1** High-flying aircraft often leave vapour trail traces of their flight paths.

Normally, we can only obtain traces of particles if the particles are electrically charged. As a fast-moving charged particle moves through matter, it tears electrons away from any atoms that it passes close to. This process, which creates positively charged ions and free electrons, is called ionisation. We can trace the path of the particle from the **ionisation** trail that it leaves behind. This is rather like the way that we trace the path of a high-flying aeroplane from the vapour trail that remains in the sky for some time after the aeroplane which caused it has gone (*figure 5.1*).

During the first half of the twentieth century, the ionisation trails of subatomic particles were captured either on **photographic film** or in **cloud chambers**. On photographic film, the ionisation trail of affected atoms in the silver halide emulsion shows up as a black trace of silver metal grains when the film is developed. In a cloud chamber, droplets of vapour condense on to a trail of ionised molecules to form a trace. The positron was discovered in 1932 using a cloud chamber (*figure 5.2*).

Most of the important discoveries in particle physics from the mid-1950s to the mid-1980s were

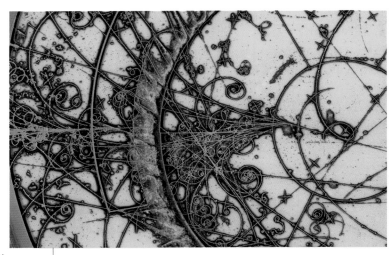

● **Figure 5.3** Particle traces in a bubble chamber.

made using the traces produced by charged particles as they passed through a **bubble chamber** (*figure 5.3*). This piece of apparatus contains liquid hydrogen at a temperature just above its boiling point, but under pressure so that it is not actually boiling. When this pressure is removed, small bubbles of hydrogen gas form around any ions that are present. This means that the ionisation trails of any charged particles leave traces in the form of lines of bubbles which can be photographed. Re-applying the pressure makes the bubbles disappear so that the bubble chamber is ready to detect more traces. Up to 30 traces per second can be recorded. Since the nucleus of a hydrogen atom comprises a single proton, the hydrogen in a bubble chamber is used both as the target at which fast-moving particles are fired and as the means of detecting the particles that are produced.

Nowadays, particle traces are obtained using various types of **electronic detector**. These provide information about particle traces millions of times per second and this information is then checked by computer for traces that are worth recording.

SAQ 5.8

List the various types of particle detector and note any particular advantages each type might have.

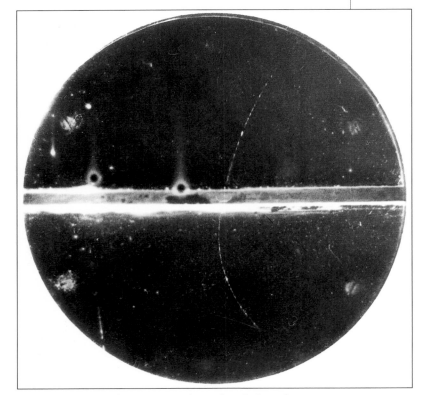

● **Figure 5.2** Positron traces in a cloud chamber.

Interpreting particle traces

Various features of the ionisation trails produced by charged particles provide evidence about the particular particles which caused them.

The particles are usually travelling at a significant fraction (i.e. at least 10%, and often much more) of the speed of light. This means that the *length* of a trace gives a good indication of the *time* that the particle producing the trace existed for.

SAQ 5.9

What can you say about the lifetime of a particle which produces a trace of **a** 5 cm, **b** 3 mm?

The main evidence for identifying particular particles is the *shape* of the traces that they produce. Particle detectors are placed in a strong magnetic field which is at right angles to the plane in which the particles are moving. The moving particles carry an electrical charge, so a force acts on them in a direction which is given by Fleming's left-hand rule (*figure 5.4*).

SAQ 5.10

What was the direction of the magnetic field that produced the positron trace shown in *figure 5.2*?

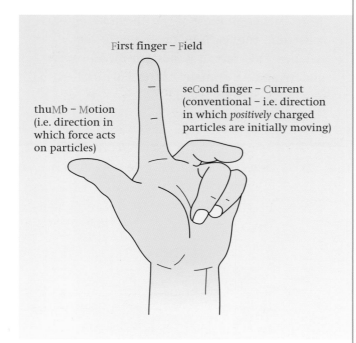

First finger – Field

seCond finger – Current (conventional – i.e. direction in which *positively* charged particles are initially moving)

thuMb – Motion (i.e. direction in which force acts on particles)

● **Figure 5.4** Fleming's left-hand rule.

Because the force acting on a particle always acts at right angles to the direction in which the particle is moving, it makes the particle move in a curved path. You can tell from the *direction* of the curve whether the charge on a particle is positive or negative. You can also tell from the *radius* of a curve what the momentum of a particle is (*box 5A*):

momentum   ∝   radius
(mass × velocity)

If the velocity of different particles in the same magnetic field is similar then:

mass   ∝   radius

A charged particle loses kinetic energy as it passes through matter and ionises atoms so its speed gradually decreases. This means that its path becomes more curved. Less massive or slow-moving particles may then produce spiral traces.

Neutral particles normally leave no traces but their existence is sometimes shown by gaps between the traces of charged particles which are part of the same series of collisions or decays.

Box 5A The path of a charged particle in a magnetic field

The force F acting on a particle with charge q, moving with speed v in a magnetic field of strength (flux density) B, is given by:

$$F = Bqv$$

[Note: The standard symbol for electrical charge is Q, but q is normally used for the charge on a single particle.]
The force F required to keep a mass m moving with a speed v in a circular path of radius r is given by:

$$F = mv^2/r$$

So for the path of a charged particle in a magnetic field:

$$Bqv = mv^2/r$$

or

$$mv = Bqr$$

For particles with the same size of charge and in the same magnetic field:

$$mv \propto r$$

[Note: Strictly, for a particle moving at a significant fraction of the speed of light, the *relativistic* mass (see *box 6C* on page 58) should be used to calculate momentum. However, the rest masses of particles travelling at roughly the same speed will still be proportional to the radius of the curves of their paths.]

SAQ 5.11

The positron whose trace is shown in *figure 5.2* passed through a lead plate.

a How does this affect the path of the positron?

b Explain why the path changes in this way.

SAQ 5.12

The two traces shown on the diagram alongside appeared in a bubble chamber at the same time. Trace A was produced by a proton. What can you say about the particle that produced trace B? Give reasons for your answer.

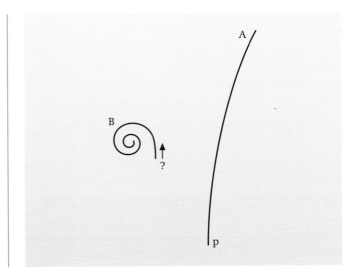

SUMMARY

◆ Energy can be changed into rest mass and rest mass can be changed into energy. The exchange rate is given by the equation:

$$E = mc^2$$

(where E is measured in J and m is measured in kg).

◆ During collisions, new particles may be produced from the kinetic energy of the colliding particles.

◆ Suitable units for measuring the energy of particles are the giga-electron-volt (GeV) and mega-electron-volt (MeV).

◆ When considering particle collisions, it is often more convenient to use the energy equivalent of each particle's mass – its rest energy – rather than the mass itself.

◆ When charged particles move through matter they cause ionisation trails. Traces of these trails can be observed on photographic film, in cloud chambers, in bubble chambers and by means of electronic detectors.

◆ The length and curvature of traces provide information about the lifetime, electrical charge, mass and speed of the particles which made them.

[Note: Although none of the above statements is listed in the learning outcomes of the syllabus, they are all important for a proper understanding of many of the learning outcomes that are listed.]

Question

1 *Figure 5.5* represents two collisions as they were visible on a bubble chamber photograph.
  These collisions were interpreted as follows:
  - first, a negative pion collides with a stationary proton:

  $$\pi^- + p^+ \rightarrow n^0 + \pi^0$$

  - then the neutron collides with another proton and changes into a further proton and a negative pion:

  $$n^0 + p^+ \rightarrow p^+ + p^+ + \pi^-$$

  [Note: The charges on the particles are important for interpreting the diagram, so they are all shown.]

  a Make a copy of the diagram, then:
    - label the point of the first collision A;
    - mark the point of the second collision B;
    - replace labels 1–5 with the symbols p^+, n^0 or π^- as appropriate.

  b Because they do not carry a charge, neither the neutron nor the neutral pion leave any trace in the bubble chamber. Explain why the path of the neutron can be identified on the diagram but the path of the π^0-particle cannot.

  c Using the data provided on page 49, calculate how much kinetic energy is lost during each of the collisions A and B. [The rest masses of a proton and a neutron are 0.938 GeV and 0.939 GeV respectively.]

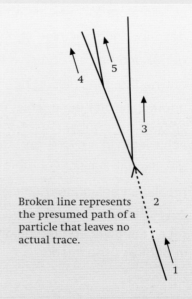

Broken line represents the presumed path of a particle that leaves no actual trace.

● **Figure 5.5** For end-of-chapter question.

Particle accelerators

By the end of this chapter you should be able to:

1 demonstrate an awareness of the use of both linear and circular particle accelerators to investigate the fundamental structure of matter;

2 describe the principles of operation of the cyclotron;

3 derive and use an equation for the supply frequency of a cyclotron;

4 outline the principles of operation of a synchrotron;

5 appreciate that the special theory of relativity places constraints upon the particle speeds achievable in all types of particle accelerator and on the particle energies achievable in a cyclotron;

6 discuss the relative advantages in the use of cyclotrons and synchrotrons;

7 recall that antimatter particles can be produced using high-energy particle accelerators;

8 recall the uses and the relative advantages of fixed targets and colliding beams in particle experiments.

How particles can be accelerated

The discoveries in particle physics described in chapters 4 and 5 all involved particles which had very high speeds and so also had, for their mass, a lot of kinetic energy. High-energy particles reach the Earth's atmosphere all the time in cosmic rays and it was through studying cosmic rays that physicists made some important discoveries of particles in the 1930s and 1940s (see pages 43 and 44). Most of the discoveries in particle physics, however, have been made using beams of high-energy particles produced in machines called **particle accelerators**.

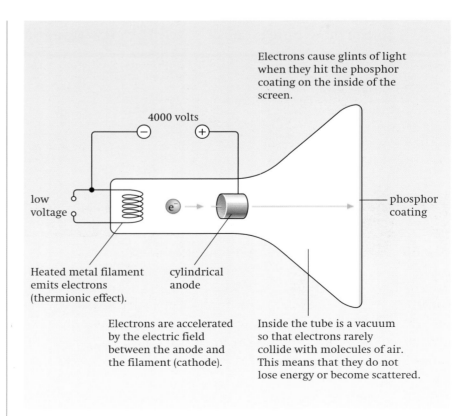

Electrons cause glints of light when they hit the phosphor coating on the inside of the screen.

4000 volts

low voltage

phosphor coating

Heated metal filament emits electrons (thermionic effect).

cylindrical anode

Electrons are accelerated by the electric field between the anode and the filament (cathode).

Inside the tube is a vacuum so that electrons rarely collide with molecules of air. This means that they do not lose energy or become scattered.

● **Figure 6.1** A simple particle accelerator.

● **Figure 6.2** The Stanford linear accelerator is 3 km long.

● **Figure 6.3** Part of the linear accelerator at Stanford.

All particle accelerators work on the same basic principle. This can conveniently be explained by looking at a simple particle accelerator that you have seen in action probably every day of your life: the cathode ray tube that produces the picture in a TV set. *Figure 6.1* shows how this works.

SAQ 6.1
Particle physics is also known as high-energy physics. Explain why.

> **Remember**
> The amount of kinetic energy transferred to an electron when it is accelerated across a potential difference of 1 volt is called an electron-volt (eV).
>
> The same amount of energy is transferred to any other particle with the same charge as an electron when it is accelerated across a potential difference of 1 volt.
>
> 1 mega-electron-volt (MeV) = 10^6 eV
> 1 giga-electron-volt (GeV) = 10^9 eV

SAQ 6.2
Particle accelerators are rated in terms of the amount of energy that they transfer to each particle that they accelerate. What is the rating – as a particle accelerator – of the TV tube shown in *figure 6.1*?

Linear accelerators (Linacs)

Linear accelerators accelerate particles along a straight line. They are basically very large versions of cathode ray tubes (*box 6A on page 56*). The linear accelerator at Stanford, in California, for example, is 3 kilometres long (*figures 6.2 and 6.3*)! It can accelerate electrons up to energies of 50 GeV. Achieving higher energies than this would require an even longer accelerator and this isn't economically feasible.

Box 6A How a linear accelerator produces high-energy electrons

The beam of electrons travels through a series of hollow, tubular electrodes.

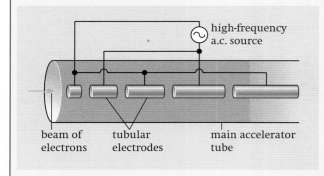

beam of electrons   tubular electrodes   main accelerator tube

high-frequency a.c. source

Each electrode is connected to the opposite side of a high-voltage, high-frequency a.c. supply from the electrodes on either side of it. Electrons are accelerated as they cross the gap between electrodes. There is no electrical field inside the tubes so the electrons travel through each tube at a steady speed. By the time they reach the next gap, the a.c. supply has gone through half a cycle. This means that the voltage across each pair of electrodes has reversed so the electrons are accelerated once again across the next gap. This happens over and over again so that by the time they have reached the end of the accelerator the electrons have reached very high speeds.

SAQ 6.3

The tubular electrodes must be longer and longer as the electrons travel down the length of a linear accelerator. Explain why.

The cyclotron

The earliest particle accelerators to produce high-energy particles were much smaller than linear accelerators. They did not accelerate particles along a straight line but in a spiral. These particle accelerators are called **cyclotrons**. The first cyclotron, which accelerated protons to a kinetic energy of 80 keV, was built in 1931 by Ernest Lawrence and a colleague. Within a year they had made a bigger machine with a rating of 1 MeV (*figure 6.4*). *Figure 6.5* shows a modern cyclotron.

The following diagram shows the main parts of a cyclotron.

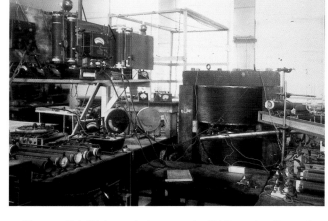

● **Figure 6.4** This cyclotron, only 27.5 cm in diameter, produced 1 MeV protons in 1932.

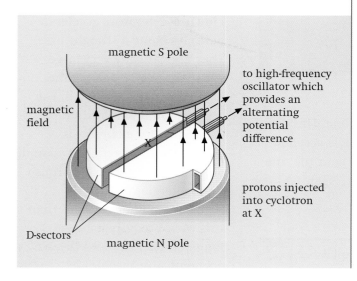

magnetic S pole

magnetic field

to high-frequency oscillator which provides an alternating potential difference

protons injected into cyclotron at X

D-sectors

magnetic N pole

● **Figure 6.5** This modern cyclotron accelerates protons to a kinetic energy of 25 MeV. The proton beam is visible because it ionises air molecules.

Protons are injected *horizontally* into the cyclotron near to the centre of the gap between the two D-sectors. Because these protons carry an electrical charge, and are moving at 90° to the direction of the magnetic field, they are acted on by a force. This force acts at 90° both to the magnetic field and to the direction in which the particles are moving (see *figure 5.4* on page 51).

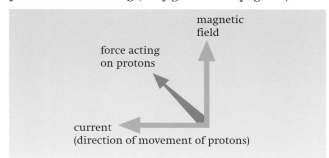

The force acting on the protons changes the direction in which they move and, since the force is *always* at 90° to the direction the protons are moving, it *keeps on* changing their direction. By itself, this centripetal force would make the protons move in a *circular* path. However, the protons in the cyclotron are also being accelerated (see below) so they do not move in a circular path but in a *spiral*.

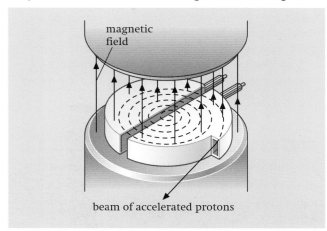

In fact, the spiral path of the protons has hundreds of loops, not just the five shown in the diagram. This means that each loop is much closer to being circular.

To accelerate the protons, there is a large potential difference between the two D-sectors. This means that protons are accelerated each time they are in the gap between the two D-sectors. An alternating potential difference is applied across the D-sectors so by the time protons have travelled halfway round the cyclotron the direction of the

potential has been reversed so that it accelerates the protons again, rather than slowing them down. In total, each proton is accelerated several hundred times before it leaves the cyclotron.

For the cyclotron to work, the time that it takes for protons to travel round a half-circuit:
- must be exactly the same at all points on the spiral;
- must be exactly the same as the time taken for a half-cycle of the alternating potential difference that is applied across the D-sectors.

The first of these conditions is met because the radius and hence the length of the path for each half-circuit is directly proportional to the speed of the protons. *Box 6B* explains how the second condition can be met.

Box 6B Calculating the a.c. supply frequency for a cyclotron

For a cyclotron to work, the alternating potential difference applied across the D-sectors must have exactly the right frequency. This frequency is called the **resonance frequency** and can be calculated as shown below.

The radius r of the path of a particle of mass m, speed v and charge q moving in a magnetic field of flux density B is given by:

$$r = \frac{mv}{Bq}$$ [See box 5A on page 51 for how to derive this relationship.]

The time t taken for a particle travelling with speed v to travel once round a circle of radius r is given by:

$$t = \frac{2\pi r}{v}$$

Combining the above two equations:

$$t = \frac{2\pi mv}{Bqv} \quad \text{i.e.} \quad t = \frac{2\pi m}{Bq}$$

[Note: The time t does not depend on either v or r. As explained earlier, this is important for the way the cyclotron works.]

To accelerate protons each time they cross the gap between the D-sectors, the applied potential difference (p.d.) must reverse twice during time t. In other words, t must be exactly equal to the period T for one full cycle of the alternating p.d.

$$T = \frac{2\pi m}{Bq}$$

The frequency f of the alternating p.d. is given by $1/T$. So:

$$f = \frac{Bq}{2\pi m}$$

The resonance frequency of a cyclotron is normally of the order of 10^7 hertz (10 MHz), i.e. it is in the radio frequency (RF) range of frequencies.

SAQ 6.4

Calculate the frequency of the alternating potential difference that must be supplied to a cyclotron which has a magnetic field with a flux density of 8.95×10^{-4} tesla (T).

SAQ 6.5

The diagram shows the path of a proton in a bubble chamber.

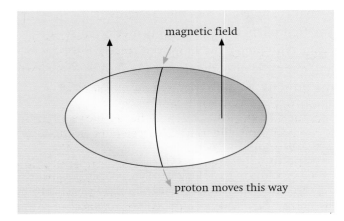

a How does this compare with the path of a proton in a cyclotron?
b How can the differences be explained?

The rating of a cyclotron can be increased to about 25 MeV by increasing its diameter. No further increase is possible because once protons are accelerated to an appreciable fraction of the speed of light the usual (Newtonian) equations of motion no longer apply. We have to use different equations based on Einstein's **special theory of relativity** (see *box 6C*). At high speeds, the effective increase in the mass of a particle starts to matter so that it takes longer to make each half-circuit of the cyclotron. This means that the alternation of the applied voltage no longer *synchronises* with the times that protons cross the gap between the D-sectors.

SAQ 6.6

At approximately what fraction of the speed of light is a proton with a kinetic energy of 25 MeV travelling? [You may use the usual formula for kinetic energy in this calculation. 1 eV = 1.602×10^{-19} J.]

Box 6C Kinetic energy and special relativity

When we accelerate a charged particle in an electric field, the work done on the particle (force × distance) is transferred to the particle as kinetic energy.

The standard formula for calculating kinetic energy E_k of a body of mass m travelling with velocity v is:

$$E_k = \tfrac{1}{2}mv^2$$

So if we plot v^2 against the work done on the particle we would expect to get a straight line.

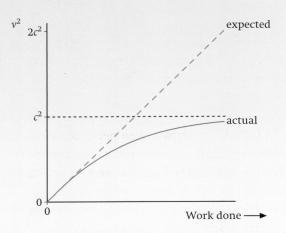

However, this is not what actually happens. Although all the work done on the particle is still transferred to the particle as kinetic energy, the velocity of the particle does not increase as much as we would expect from the formula $E_k = \tfrac{1}{2}mv^2$. This means that the standard formula for kinetic energy, though it gives a very good approximation for low velocities, is incorrect.

According to Einstein's special theory of relativity, kinetic energy should be calculated using the relationship:

$$E_k = mc^2 \left(\frac{1}{\sqrt{1 - v^2/c^2}} - 1 \right)$$

SAQ 6.7

You can see from the graph that as the amount of work done on a particle increases, its velocity gets closer and closer to a certain limiting value without ever quite getting there. What is this limiting velocity?

SAQ 6.8

a Use Einstein's formula to calculate E_k for any body when:
   (i) $v = 0$;   (ii) $v = c$.
b Work out what Einstein's formula for E_k becomes when v is small, i.e. when:

$$\frac{1}{\sqrt{1 - v^2/c^2}} - 1 \approx 1 + \tfrac{1}{2}v^2/c^2$$

The synchrotron

The limitation imposed by the special theory of relativity on the particle speeds and energies that can be produced by cyclotrons led to the development of a type of particle accelerator called a **synchrotron** (*figures 6.6 to 6.8*).

In a synchrotron, magnetic fields are used to make a batch of charged particles travel many times around a circular path. The particles are accelerated by electrical fields each time they pass through various regions (cavities) around the circle. As the speed of the particles increases:

■ the strength of the magnetic fields keeping them in their circular path also needs to be increased;

■ the frequency of the alternating potential difference applied across the accelerating cavities needs to be increased so that the direction of the potential difference across each cavity is *synchronised* with when the particles are passing through it.

The problem with synchrotrons, as with any other type of circular accelerator, is that the charged particles must constantly be accelerated towards the centre of the circle simply to keep them moving in a circular path. Whenever charged particles are accelerated they emit electromagnetic radiation. So the particles moving in a circular path around a synchrotron constantly emit energy in the form of radiation. Because the particles are constantly losing energy in this way, quite a lot of

● **Figure 6.7** At CERN (Conseil Européen pour la Recherche Nucléaire) near Geneva:
■ the 4.25 km radius circle is the LEP (large electron – positron collider) which accelerates electrons and positrons to kinetic energies of 50 GeV;
■ the 1.1 km radius circle is the SPS (super proton synchrotron) which accelerates protons and antiprotons to kinetic energies of 450 GeV.
[The dotted line is the Swiss–French border.]

the work done on the particles in the accelerator does not *increase* the kinetic energy of the particles but is used simply to *maintain* it. The acceleration needed to keep a particle moving in a circle is inversely proportional to the radius of the circle (see *box 5A* on page 52). Synchrotrons are, therefore, built with a large radius in order to reduce the problem of energy losses due to radiation.

[Note: Some synchrotrons are built specifically to *produce* short-wavelength electromagnetic radiation which can be used, for example, to study the structure of materials.]

The special theory of relativity (see *box 6C*) tells us that there is a limit to the *speed* to which particles can be accelerated in synchrotrons, because they can never reach the speed of light. There is, however, no *theoretical* limit to the *kinetic energy* which can be transferred to particles. There is, however, a *practical* limit because of the size and the cost of the synchrotrons that would be needed to accelerate them.

● **Figure 6.6** The Fermilab synchrotron in Chicago has a radius of 1 km. It can accelerate protons to a kinetic energy of almost 1000 GeV, so it is called a teratron.

SAQ 6.9

Explain the name *synchrotron*.

SAQ 6.10

Explain the differences in the diameters of, and the energies achieved by, the LEP and SPS at CERN. [You will find the relevant information on the illustrations on page 59.]

Synchrotrons can achieve far higher particle energies than cyclotrons and are, therefore, more useful for experiments concerned with investigating fundamental particles. But the lower-energy beams of particles produced by cyclotrons are more continuous, have a higher particle density and have a narrower band of energies than the bursts of particles produced by synchrotrons. These characteristics make cyclotrons more useful for some purposes than synchrotrons. Historically, for example, cyclotrons were used to establish the structure of many atomic nuclei. Small cyclotrons, roughly the same size as a small car, are still used in hospitals (*figure 6.9*), e.g. to produce beams of α-particles for treating eye cancer and to produce radionuclides for use in radiotherapy and certain types of imaging.

Fixed targets versus colliding beams

Fixed target experiments

Beams of high-energy particles may be fired at **fixed targets**, e.g. a proton target such as liquid hydrogen. If the liquid hydrogen is in a bubble chamber, it can also be used to form traces of the paths of the particles that are produced by the collisions (see page 51).

● **Figure 6.8** Inside the accelerator of the CERN SPS.

Fixed targets have the advantage that they are made up from densely packed particles. This means that there is a very good chance (high probability) of high-energy particles colliding with the target as they pass through it.

A serious disadvantage of fixed targets, however, is that only part of the kinetic energy of particles in the beam is available for creating new particles as a result of collisions. This is because there must always be the same overall amount of momentum after a collision as there was before. Momentum must be conserved.

The momentum of a particle is given by the relationship:

momentum = mass × velocity

[Strictly, according to the special theory of relativity, the relativistic mass $m_0 / \sqrt{[1 - v^2/c^2]}$ should be used, where m_0 is the rest mass of the particle.]

● **Figure 6.9** A cyclotron used in a hospital.

A fast-moving particle has a lot of momentum but a particle in a fixed target with which the moving particle collides has zero momentum. This means that the total momentum of all the particles that emerge from the collision must be the same as the momentum of the original fast-moving particle. After the collision, therefore, at least some of the particles must have some momentum. If they have momentum, they must have velocity, and if they have velocity, they must have kinetic energy. This kinetic energy cannot, therefore, be available during the collision, for creating new mass.

Consider, for example, the following collision reaction which is used to produce antiprotons by accelerating protons to an energy of 6.4 GeV and then making them collide with a stationary hydrogen target:

$$p^+ \quad + \quad p^+ \quad \rightarrow \quad p^+ + p^+ + p^+ + p^-$$

stationary	from beam	Assume for simplicity that each has momentum of $\frac{1}{4}mv$ in the same direction as proton from beam

*Momentum: $\quad mv \qquad 4 \times \frac{1}{4}mv = mv$

*Kinetic energy: $\quad \frac{1}{2}mv^2 \qquad 4 \times \frac{1}{2}m(v/4)^2 = \frac{1}{2}mv^2 \times \frac{1}{4}$

[*Note: Non-relativistic formulae have been used for simplicity.]

Although not strictly accurate, the above calculation shows that a maximum of about 75% of the kinetic energy from the moving proton would be available for the creation of new matter. In practice, it would be considerably less than this, especially at high particle speeds.

SAQ 6.11

Suppose that the collision between a moving proton and a stationary proton produced the following:

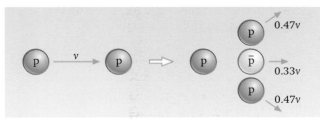

Using non-relativistic formulae, calculate the percentage of the moving proton's kinetic energy which is available to create new matter.

Colliding beam experiments

The problem that not much of the kinetic energy of a high-energy particle is available to create new matter in collisions can be overcome by making two beams of moving particles collide with each other. These are called **colliding beam** experiments.

For example, a beam of antiprotons can be accelerated in a synchrotron and then made to collide with a beam of protons which have been accelerated to the same speed, but in the opposite direction, in the same synchrotron. (It is possible to arrange the magnetic fields to keep the particles apart until they have been accelerated to their maximum velocity.)

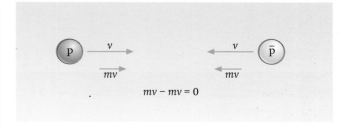

The total momentum of two colliding particles is now zero. So although the particles resulting from the collision are likely to have *some* kinetic energy, much more of the energy of the colliding particles is available for the production of new matter. Furthermore, since *both* of the colliding particles have been accelerated until they have the maximum kinetic energy that the synchrotron can provide, the available energy is effectively doubled.

SAQ 6.12

The CERN LEP (*figure 6.7*) is used for electron–positron collisions. The Fermilab teratron (*figure 6.6*) is used for proton–antiproton collisions. What is the effective energy of each of these collisions?

When relativity is taken into account, as it must be with high-energy particles, the energy advantages of colliding beam experiments are even greater. Colliding beams each with particle energies of just over 45 MeV, for example, could produce very massive particles with a rest energy of 90 MeV. To produce these particles using a fixed target would require a 4500 GeV beam of particles.

Colliding beam experiments do, however, have some disadvantages. The collision rate, for example, is a lot lower. A bundle of particles in a beam typically contains about 10^{11} particles per cm^2 cross-section whereas a liquid hydrogen target contains around 10^{25} protons per cm^2.

SAQ 6.13
How many times greater is the chance of a collision with a fixed target than with colliding beams?

To mitigate this problem of a low collision rate, colliding beams are focused into a small cross-sectional area. Bundles of particles can also be collected into a storage ring and kept circulating until plenty have accumulated. The collision rate can be increased by these methods so that it is only about 10^6 times lower than in fixed target reactions.

SUMMARY

◆ Scientists investigate the fundamental structure of matter using beams of high-energy particles produced in particle accelerators.

◆ Charged particles are accelerated using electrical fields; to give particles very high speeds and correspondingly high kinetic energies, they need to be accelerated over and over again.

◆ In linear accelerators, particles are accelerated along a straight line; to achieve high speeds, linear accelerators need to be very long.

◆ Magnetic fields can be used to make parti-·cles move in a circular path. The particles can then be accelerated by electrical fields each time they pass certain points around the circle.

◆ In a cyclotron, the radius of a particle's path increases with its speed so it moves in a spiral. But the time taken for a particle to make one circuit stays the same. This means that an alternating potential difference applied across the D-sectors can be used to accelerate the particles each time they cross the gap between the sectors. For this to happen, the alternating p.d. must have a frequency of $Bq/2\pi m$. [You must be able to *derive* and to *use* this formula.]

◆ The effective mass of a particle increases with its speed in accordance with the special theory of relativity. This limits the speed to which particles can be accelerated in a cyclotron.

◆ In a synchrotron, particles move many times around a circular path. The strength of the magnetic fields (which keep particles moving in a circular path) and the frequency of the alternating potential difference (which accelerates them) both need to be increased as the speed of the particles increases.

◆ Though relativity imposes an upper limit on the speed of particles, there is no limit, other than size and cost, on the kinetic energy that can be transferred to particles in a synchrotron.

When beams of particles are fired at fixed targets, momentum must be conserved so that the particles present after a collision possess kinetic energy. This energy is not, therefore, available to produce new matter.

In colliding beam experiments, pairs of colliding particles have no overall momentum so most of the kinetic energy of both particles is available to produce new matter.

The low rate of collisions in colliding beam experiments can be increased by focusing beams and by accumulating particles in storage rings.

Fixed targets are used to produce the anti-matter particles which are then used in colliding beam experiments.

Questions

1 In November 1974, two teams of particle physicists, in the USA, independently discovered the J/ψ (psi) hadron with a rest energy of 3.1 GeV:
- a team led by Samuel Ting fired high-energy protons at a fixed beryllium target;
- a team led by Burton Richter used an electron–positron colliding beam reaction.

a How does the mass of the J/ψ hadron compare with the mass of a proton?

b What would you expect the kinetic energy of the electrons and positrons in Richter's colliding beam experiment to have been?

c How would the kinetic energy of Ting's protons have compared with the kinetic energy of the electrons and positrons in Richter's experiment?

2 a Compare the scale of large particle accelerators with the scale of the particles they are used to discover.

b Large particle accelerators cost several billion pounds to build and hundreds of millions of pounds each year to run. Is this cost justified given the conflicting demands for money for other services, such as education, health care, aid to developing countries, the arts or space programmes?

[Rest mass/energy of a proton is 0.938 GeV.]

CHAPTER 7

Making sense of hadrons

By the end of this chapter you should be able to:

1 recall that electrical charge is conserved during hadron reactions (decay and interactions);

2 recall that there are two types of hadron: baryons and mesons;

3 recall that protons and neutrons are baryons with a baryon number of 1 and that antiprotons and antineutrons are baryons with a baryon number of −1;

4 recall that baryon number is conserved during hadron reactions and that if the number of baryons changes this is because baryon particle–antiparticle pairs are created or annihilated;

5 recall that the number of mesons is not necessarily conserved during hadron reactions;

6 recall that protons and neutrons cannot themselves be fundamental particles because they contain smaller charged particles called quarks;

7 describe a simple quark model in terms of up, down and strange quarks, plus their respective antiquarks, taking into account their charge, baryon number and strangeness;

8 describe the properties of protons and neutrons in terms of a simple quark model;

9 appreciate that the quark model can be extended to include the properties of charm, bottomness and topness;

10 recall that the properties of all hadrons may be described in terms of the extended quark model.

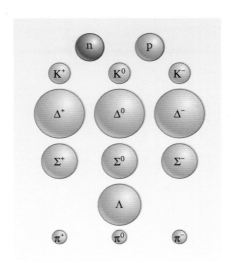

● **Figure 7.1** Some hadrons.

Finding patterns in hadron reactions

As described in chapter 4, by the early 1960s scientists had discovered over 100 different hadrons (*figure 7.1*) and many thousands of different reactions between colliding hadrons. When faced with this bewildering diversity of data, scientists tried – as scientists always do – to make better sense of it by looking for *patterns*. In fact, they had already made significant progress along this road during the 1950s.

The following equations show three hadron reactions that you have already met in previous chapters (see pages 47, 48 and 53):

$$p^+ + p^+ \rightarrow p^+ + p^+ + \pi^0$$
$$p^+ + n^0 \rightarrow p^+ + p^+ + \pi^-$$
$$\pi^- + p^+ \rightarrow n^0 + \pi^0$$

[Note: The charges on protons and neutrons have been shown to make it easier to spot patterns.]

If you look carefully at even this very small number of reactions, you can see some patterns:

- the total amount of electrical charge before and after a reaction remains the same – electrical charge is **conserved**;
- reactions can produce extra pions that weren't there before;
- although protons and neutrons can each appear or disappear, the total number of nucleons (protons + neutrons) remains the same.

When particle physicists looked at many more reactions, involving many more types of hadron, they confirmed that electrical charge is always conserved.

They also found that:

- the total number of some types of hadron, including protons and neutrons, is normally the same after a reaction as it was before the reaction;
- the total number of other types of hadron, including pions, is often different after a reaction than it was before the reaction.

These two types of hadrons were called **baryons** and **mesons** respectively (*box 7A*).

In hadron interactions:

- the total number of baryons normally remains the same;
- the total number of mesons may change.

SAQ 7.1 _____

Protons, pions and neutrons are all hadrons. Which of these particles are:

a baryons;

b mesons?

There are, however, some hadron reactions where there is a *different* number of baryons after the reaction than there were before the reaction. For example, two protons can collide to produce a further proton plus an antiproton:

$$p + p \rightarrow p + p + p + \bar{p}$$

Notice, however, that the extra baryon, p (a proton), is accompanied by its antiparticle, $\bar{p}$ (an antiproton). In fact, whenever an extra baryon is created in a hadron reaction, the corresponding antibaryon is also created.

If we give all baryons a baryon number of +1 and all antibaryons a baryon number of −1, the following rule then applies to *all* hadron reactions:

The total **baryon number** is always the same before and after a hadron reaction. In other words, baryon number is conserved.

To summarise, during the 1950s, particle physicists divided hadrons into two groups – baryons and mesons – and discovered two rules about hadron reactions:

Rule 1 Electrical charge is conserved.
Rule 2 Baryon number is conserved.

Box 7A Two types of hadron

Baryons ($B = 1$)		Mesons ($B = 0$)	
delta-plus	Δ^+	kay*-plus	K^+
delta-zero	Δ^0	kay*-zero	K^0
delta-minus	Δ^-	kay*-minus	K^-
lambda	Λ	phi	ϕ
neutron	n^0	pi-plus	π^+
proton	p^+	pi-zero	π^0
sigma-plus	Σ^+	pi-minus	π^-
sigma-zero	Σ^0		
sigma-minus	Σ^-		
		[* or kappa]	

Notes

1 The corresponding antibaryons have the opposite electrical charge and a baryon number of −1.

2 When you do SAQ 7.7 on page 68 you will understand how a *neutral* hadron can have an antiparticle with the opposite electrical charge.

SAQ 7.2

Here are two more reactions that you met in an earlier chapter:

$$\Delta^- \rightarrow n^0 + \pi^-$$
$$\Sigma^+ \rightarrow p^+ + \pi^0$$

Are Δ^--particles and Σ^+ particles baryons or mesons? Give reasons for your answer.

[Note: These are hadron *decays* rather than hadron *collisions*, but in these cases the same rules apply.]

The two rules about hadron reactions can be used to decide whether or not a particular hadron reaction can occur (see *box 7B*).

Box 7B How to decide whether or not a hadron reaction can occur

To decide whether or not a hadron reaction can occur, it is best to set out the electrical charges and baryon numbers as follows:

Example 1

$$p^+ + p^+ \rightarrow p^+ + p^+ + \pi^+ + \pi^- ?$$

Q (charge) $(+1) + (+1)$ $(+1) + (+1) + (+1) + (-1)$
total +2 total +2
i.e. Q is conserved

B (baryon $(+1) + (+1)$ $(+1) + (+1) + 0 + 0$
number) total +2 total +2
i.e. B is conserved

Q and B are both conserved ∴ reaction can happen

Example 2

$$p^+ + p^+ \rightarrow p^+ + p^+ + n^0 ?$$

Q (charge) $(+1) + (+1)$ $(+1) + (+1) + 0$
total +2 total +2
i.e. Q is conserved

B (baryon $(+1) + (+1)$ $(+1) + (+1) + (+1)$
number) total +2 total +3
i.e. B is *not* conserved

Q is conserved but B is not ∴ reaction cannot happen

SAQ 7.3

Which of the following reactions cannot happen? In each case give a reason for your answer.

a $\pi^- + p^+ \rightarrow K^+ + \Sigma^-$
b $n^0 + p^+ \rightarrow n^0 + p^+ + p^+ + \pi^-$
c $\Sigma^+ \rightarrow \Lambda + \pi^-$
d $p^+ + p^+ \rightarrow \pi^- + p^+ + n^0$

When they were using the two rules, scientists were puzzled to find that some reactions that were 'allowed' by the rules did not, in fact, ever happen. For example:

$$p^+ + p^+ \rightarrow p^+ + \Sigma^+ + \pi^0$$

Q $(+1) + (+1)$ $(+1) + (+1) + 0$
total +2 total +2

B $(+1) + (+1)$ $(+1) + (+1) + 0$
total +2 total +2

Q and B both conserved ∴ reaction can happen

Scientists also discovered that the reactions which did not happen always involved certain hadrons – for example, Λ, Σ and K – that were different from most others in some ways. These hadrons were unstable like most other hadrons but decayed more slowly (they had half-lives of around 10^{-10} s rather than the more usual 10^{-23} s).

It was also found that these hadrons were never created singly but always in pairs. The following reaction, for example, does occur:

$$p^+ + p^+ \rightarrow p^+ + \underbrace{\Sigma^+ + K^0}$$
pair of 'strange' hadrons

To account for the strange behaviour of these hadrons, particle physicists realised that there must be another property, besides electrical charge and baryon number, which hadrons can possess. They called this new property **strangeness**. Strangeness is normally conserved in hadron reactions.

Of the hadrons listed in *box 7A*, only those shown in *box 7C* have any strangeness; the other baryons and mesons shown in the earlier table have a strangeness value (S) of zero.

Box 7C Strangeness values of some hadrons

Baryons	S	Mesons	S
Λ	−1	K^+	+1
Σ^+	−1	K^0	+1
Σ^0	−1	K^-	+1
Σ^-	−1		

SAQ 7.4

a Use strangeness values to show why the reaction:

$$p^+ + p^+ \rightarrow p^+ + \Sigma^+ + \pi^0$$

cannot happen.

b Use Q, B and S values to show that the reaction:

$$p^+ + p^+ \rightarrow p^+ + \Sigma^+ + K^0$$

can happen.

c Decide whether each of the following reactions can, or cannot, happen. Give your reasons in each case.
(i) $K^+ + p^+ \rightarrow \pi^+ + \Sigma^+$
(ii) $K^- + p^+ \rightarrow \pi^+ + \Sigma^-$

Explaining the patterns in hadron reactions

In 1964, Murray Gell-Mann and George Zweig independently came up with the same model to explain the patterns they and other particle physicists had found in hadron reactions.

They both suggested that hadrons are not, in fact, *fundamental* particles at all, but are themselves made up of even smaller particles. Gell-Mann called these smaller particles 'quarks' and Zweig called them 'aces', but it was the former name which stuck (*box 7D*).

The quark model of hadrons

In the basic quark model, all hadrons – baryons, antibaryons and mesons – are made up from just three types or **flavours** of quark. At one time physicists were seriously thinking of naming the three types of quark after three common flavours of ice-cream – chocolate, strawberry and vanilla. Eventually, however, sanity (or timidity) prevailed and physicists settled on the names **up** (**u**), **down** (**d**) and **strange** (**s**). But the idea of different flavours stuck and we still use the term today.

The electrical charges, baryon numbers and strangeness values of these quarks are shown in *table 7.1*.

Quark (flavour)	Charge (Q)	Baryon number (B)	Strangeness (S)
u	$+\frac{2}{3}$	$+\frac{1}{3}$	0
d	$-\frac{1}{3}$	$+\frac{1}{3}$	0
s	$-\frac{1}{3}$	$+\frac{1}{3}$	−1

● **Table 7.1** Q, B and S values for up, down and strange quarks.

The three antiquarks, $\bar{u}$, $\bar{d}$ and $\bar{s}$, were given the *opposite* values of Q, B and S to those possessed by the corresponding quarks.

SAQ 7.5

Make a similar table to the one above for the properties of the three antiquarks.

Box 7D Where did the word *quark* come from?

Murray Gell-Mann originally *invented* the name 'qu**o**rk' for the particles from which hadrons are made because he wanted a *meaningless* name. This was because the meaningful names which had previously been used for particles had turned out to be wrong. For example, atoms ('indivisible ones') could, in fact, be split up into smaller particles and there are mesons ('middleweights') which are more massive than some baryons ('heavyweights').

Gell-Mann then discovered the (also meaningless) word 'quark' in James Joyce's weird novel *Finnegan's Wake*:

'... *Three quarks for Muster Mark.*
Sure he hasn't got much of a bark
And sure any he has it's all beside the mark.'

and so he adopted the spelling that is now used. So 'quark' is a quirky name, taken from a quirky novel, for some pretty quirky particles!

Murray Gell-Mann.

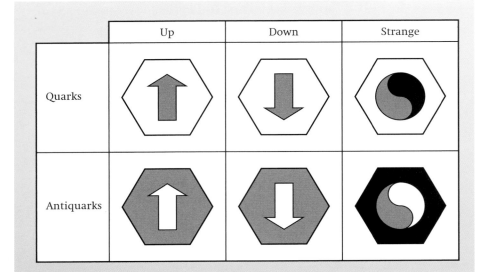

● **Figure 7.2** Icons for up, down and strange quarks and their corresponding antiquarks.

In order to see more strikingly which quarks and antiquarks are contained in which baryons, antibaryons and mesons the icons in *figure 7.2* will often be used.

Baryons

Each baryon consists of three quarks which may be combined in any way, i.e. all the same flavour, two the same flavour or all different flavours. For example:

$$
\begin{array}{lllll}
\text{proton} & = & \{u & u & d\} \\
Q & +1 & = & (+\frac{2}{3}) + (+\frac{2}{3}) + (-\frac{1}{3}) \\
B & +1 & = & (+\frac{1}{3}) + (+\frac{1}{3}) + (+\frac{1}{3}) \\
S & 0 & = & 0 + 0 + 0
\end{array}
$$

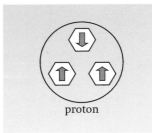

proton

An antiproton consists of the three corresponding antiquarks:

$$\{\bar{u}\ \bar{u}\ \bar{d}\}$$

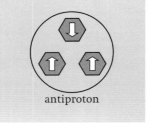

antiproton

Mesons

Each meson consists of a quark and an antiquark. These may be the same flavour or different flavours. For example:

$$
\begin{array}{lllll}
& \pi^{+} & = & \{u & \bar{d}\} \\
Q & +1 & = & +\frac{2}{3} & + & +\frac{1}{3} \\
B & 0 & = & +\frac{1}{3} & + & -\frac{1}{3} \\
S & 0 & = & 0 & + & 0
\end{array}
$$

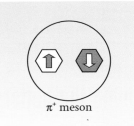

π^{+} meson

SAQ 7.6

Show, in a similar way to the previous examples, that:
a the baryon made from the quarks {u d d} has the properties of a neutron;
b a meson consisting of the quarks {u $\bar{s}$} has the properties of a K^{+}-particle.

SAQ 7.7

A neutron and an antineutron can be said to have opposite electrical charges even though neither has any overall charge. Explain how this is possible.

Box 7E The quark composition of some hadrons

Baryons	Quarks	Mesons	Quarks
Δ^{+}	{u u d}	K^{+}	{u $\bar{s}$}
Δ^{0}	{u d d}	K^{0}	{d $\bar{s}$}
Δ^{-}	{d d d}	K^{-}	{s $\bar{u}$}
Λ	{u d s}	ϕ (phi)	{s $\bar{s}$}
n^{0}	{u d d}	π^{+}	{u $\bar{d}$}
p^{+}	{u u d}	π^{0}	{u $\bar{u}$} or {d $\bar{d}$}
Σ^{+}	{u u s}	π^{-}	{d $\bar{u}$}
Σ^{0}	{u d s}		
Σ^{-}	{d d s}		

Although the quark model of hadrons (see *box 7E*) explained their observed properties very well, many physicists were concerned that no separate quarks had ever been seen in experiments. The quark model had to be able to provide a reasonable explanation for this.

Why we never see separate quarks

Supporters of the quark model of hadrons suggested that we never see separate quarks because of the forces that hold them together inside hadrons. The quarks appear to be relatively free of each other when inside hadrons. However, if the quarks are being pulled apart for any reason, for example during a collision, the force between them becomes very strong. This means that the energy that is needed to pull a quark out of a hadron is always enough to create an additional quark+antiquark pair. So when you try to pull a hadron apart you never get a separate quark; you always end up with an *extra* hadron (in fact, a meson) instead (see *figure 7.3*).

Explaining hadron collision reactions

If you set out hadron reactions as shown below, you can then see what is happening in the reaction at the level of quarks.

$$p^+ + p^+ \rightarrow p^+ + p^+ + \pi^0$$

u	u	u	u	u
u	u	u	u	ū
d	d	d	d	

In this reaction, the kinetic energy of the collision has created a new quark+antiquark pair, {u ū}, which forms a pi-zero meson.

SAQ 7.8

Write out the following reaction, showing the quark structure of all the hadrons as in the example above:

$$p^+ + p^+ \rightarrow p^+ + n^0 + \pi^+$$

a What quark+antiquark pair has been created in this reaction?

b What else has happened in the reaction?

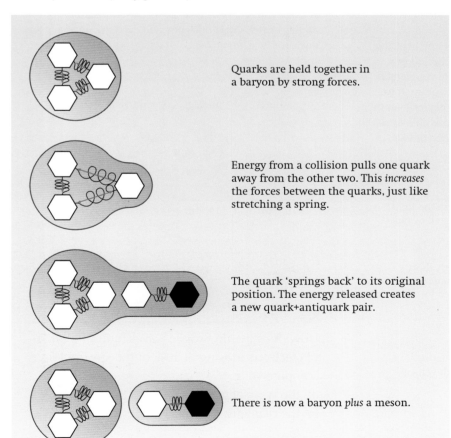

Quarks are held together in a baryon by strong forces.

Energy from a collision pulls one quark away from the other two. This *increases* the forces between the quarks, just like stretching a spring.

The quark 'springs back' to its original position. The energy released creates a new quark+antiquark pair.

There is now a baryon *plus* a meson.

Box 7F Why 'strange' hadrons always appear in pairs

When two zero-strangeness particles collide, either no strange quarks are produced or a strange quark+antiquark pair is produced.

If the strange quark and the strange antiquark end up in the same hadron, it will have zero strangeness.

If the strange quark and the strange antiquark end up in different hadrons there will then be *two* strange hadrons.

The +1 and −1 strangenesses of these two hadrons will, however, balance so that strangeness is conserved in the reaction overall.

[Note: When strange particles *decay*, however, strangeness may *not* be conserved. This is dealt with in chapter 8.]

● **Figure 7.3** What happens if you try to separate quarks.

Hadron reactions can be regarded as colliding 'bags' of quarks. At the moment of collision:

- quarks can be exchanged between bags;
- new quark+antiquark pairs can be created from the kinetic energy of the colliding particles;
- a quark and an antiquark can annihilate each other, releasing energy.

When a new quark+antiquark pair is created, the quark and antiquark are always the same flavour. For example, an up quark and an anti-up quark may be created, or a down quark and an anti-down quark, but *not* an up quark and an anti-down quark. In other words:

During hadron reactions, **flavour is conserved.**

Direct experimental evidence for the quark model

As a scientific theory, the quark model is a huge success. It explains the properties of hadrons and the outcomes of collisions between hadrons with admirable ease and simplicity. But scientists are rarely satisfied with a model simply because it works; they prefer to have some direct experimental evidence that entities in their models – in this case quarks – really do exist. In fact, experimental evidence for the existence of quarks was found during the second half of the 1960s, shortly after the quark model of hadrons had first been put forward.

Box 7G Using electron beams as a microscope

In 1925, Louis de Broglie showed that something very surprising followed from Einstein's theories about electromagnetic waves travelling as small packets (quanta) of energy called photons and about mass and energy being interchangeable. He showed that moving particles of matter can behave like waves. This means that small, fast-moving particles such as electrons can be used instead of light to 'see' things with.

To be able to see an object with waves of any type, the waves must strike the object and then be reflected or scattered from it. This can only happen if the wavelength of the waves is smaller than the object that you wish to see. The wavelength of ordinary light is far bigger than the diameter of atoms. This means that it is impossible to see atoms with ordinary light no matter how powerful a microscope you have.

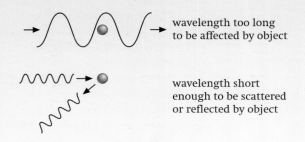

wavelength too long to be affected by object

wavelength short enough to be scattered or reflected by object

De Broglie showed that the effective wavelength (λ) of particles of matter with mass m moving with velocity v is given by:

$$\lambda = h/mv$$

[Note: h has the value 6.626×10^{-34} J s and is known as the Planck constant.]

[Max Planck came up with the idea that radiation is emitted in definite 'chunks' (quanta) in 1900, five years

before Einstein's work on the photoelectric effect. Planck did not, however, think that light and other types of electromagnetic radiation actually consisted of 'energy particles'. He regarded his idea simply as a way of calculating values which matched the measurements made of the radiation emitted by hot objects.]

Electrons have only a very small mass and, if they are moving fast enough their effective (de Broglie) wavelength is short enough to be able to 'see' not only atoms, but atomic nuclei, single nucleons and even the quarks inside nucleons (see *figure 7.4*).

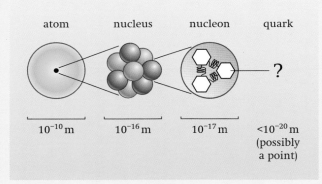

atom	nucleus	nucleon	quark
10^{-10} m	10^{-16} m	10^{-17} m	$<10^{-20}$ m (possibly a point)

● **Figure 7.4**

SAQ 7.9

How does the de Broglie wavelength of a beam of electrons moving at 10% of the speed of light compare with:

a the wavelength of light (4 to 8×10^{-7} m);

b the diameter of a proton?

(Mass of electron = 9.1×10^{-31} kg; speed of light = 3×10^8 m s^{-1})

High-energy electrons produced by the Stanford linear accelerator (see chapter 6) were fired at protons. The idea behind this experiment was not to create new particles but to explore the detailed structure of protons. The high-energy electron beam was being used as a super-microscope (see *box 7G*).

The way the electrons were scattered (diffracted) in this experiment confirmed earlier evidence that protons have a definite size, rather than being concentrated at a single point. The scattering also indicated that protons were not simply uniform spheres but that there were point-like entities inside each proton where electrical charges were concentrated. Furthermore the results were consistent with these charges being $+\frac{2}{3}$, $+\frac{2}{3}$ and $-\frac{1}{3}$ compared to the charge of an electron of -1 and the overall charge on a proton of $+1$. In other words, protons really do seem to be made up of quarks as proposed by Gell-Mann and Zweig.

Extending the quark model

Particle physicists soon realised that the three-quark model needed to be extended. One of the reasons for this was the need, in the detailed theory of the model, for **symmetry**, i.e. to have the same number of quarks as there are **leptons**, the family of fundamental particles to which the electron belongs. (Leptons are considered in detail in chapter 8.)

In the mid-1960s, four leptons were known to exist so it was strongly suspected that a fourth quark must also exist. Particle physicists called this fourth quark **charm** (**c**). In 1974, a $\{c\,\bar{c}\}$ meson called **J/ψ** (J/psi) was discovered independently by two research teams in the USA (see question 1 at the end of chapter 6). This meson had a rest energy of 3.1 GeV, i.e. it was more than three times as massive as a proton.

	J/ψ		{c	$\bar{c}$}
Q	0	=	$(+\frac{2}{3})$ +	$(-\frac{2}{3})$
B	0	=	$(+\frac{1}{3})$ +	$(-\frac{1}{3})$
S	0	=	0 +	0
C	0	=	$(+1)$ +	(-1)

The J/ψ meson consists of a charm quark plus a charm antiquark, so it has an overall charm value of zero. During 1975 and 1976, other mesons were discovered which contained only one charm quark (or antiquark). These mesons do have a net overall charm value, or **naked** charm.

The discovery of more, and more massive, leptons then led to the search for more, and more massive, quarks. In 1977, a new meson with a large rest energy of 9 GeV, and believed to contain a quark+antiquark pair known as **bottom (b)**, was discovered. Soon afterwards mesons with a net overall bottomness – naked bottom! – were also discovered. A sixth quark, known as **top (t)**, was also thought to exist but was not discovered until 1994. Since the top quark appears to have a rest mass 35 times greater than the next most massive quark (bottom), it isn't surprising that the $\{t\,\bar{t}\}$ meson proved to be difficult to create. Icons can also be used for these quarks/antiquarks (*figure 7.5*).

Are quarks fundamental particles?

Atoms were once thought to be fundamental particles, but then it was found that atoms were made up of electrons, protons and neutrons.

Then particle physicists found that protons and neutrons were not fundamental particles either. They were just two of many types of hadron all of which are made up of smaller particles called quarks. So the question naturally arises: are quarks *really* fundamental particles?

	Charm	Bottom	Top
Quarks			
Antiquarks			

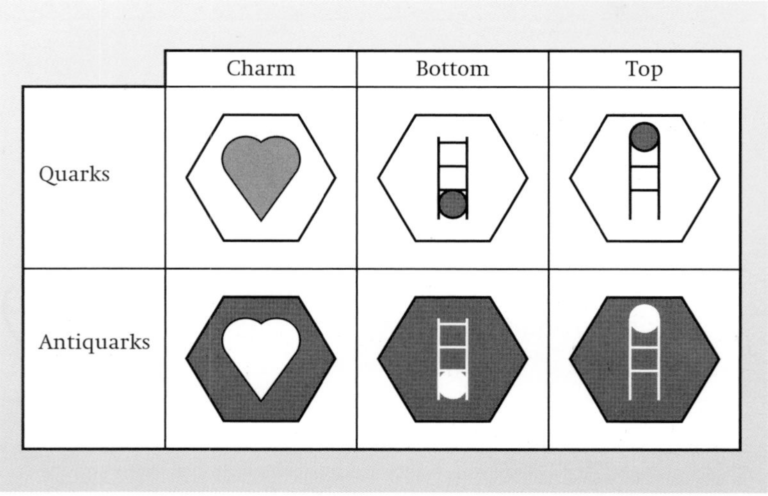

● **Figure 7.5** Icons for charm, bottom and top quarks and their corresponding antiquarks.

Despite the cautionary tale outlined above, many physicists believe that quarks might well be fundamental. The main reason for this belief is the fact that we never find separate individual quarks but always find them **confined** inside hadrons, in pairs (mesons) or in groups of three (baryons). Perhaps this is because they really are fundamental particles. Even if they are not, the confinement of quarks inside hadrons probably means that we shall never know!

SUMMARY

◆ There are two types of hadron: baryons (including protons and neutrons) with a baryon number of 1, and mesons with a baryon number of 0.

◆ During hadron reactions, electrical charge, baryon number and strangeness are all conserved.

◆ The properties and reactions of hadrons can be explained if hadrons consist of smaller particles called quarks.

◆ In the basic quark model there are three flavours of quark, up, down and strange, plus the corresponding antiquarks.

◆ Baryons consist of three quarks which may be the same flavour or different flavours; antibaryons consist of three antiquarks.

◆ Mesons consist of quark+antiquark pairs which may be the same flavour or different flavours.

◆ Separate quarks are never observed; they are always found confined in hadrons.

◆ Attempts to separate quarks may result in the creation of new quark+antiquark pairs which both have the same flavour.

◆ In hadron collisions, quarks may be exchanged between hadrons and/or new quark+antiquark pairs may be created.

◆ Quarks may be 'seen' inside hadrons using beams of high-energy electrons which have a sufficiently small effective (de Broglie) wavelength.

◆ Theory suggests, and observation confirms, that there are three further flavours of quark: charm, bottom and top.

◆ Quarks *may* be truly fundamental particles.

Questions

1 Gell-Mann predicted the existence of a hadron made up of three strange quarks. This particle, Ω^-, was first observed in 1964 in the traces produced by the following collision:

$$K^- + p^+ \rightarrow K^0 + K^+ + \Omega^- \text{ (omega-minus)}$$

a Write down the particle equation given above, and underneath show the quarks in each particle.

b What extra quarks have been created? Explain how these were produced.

c What quarks have disappeared? What do you think has happened to them?

2 a Write down the following equation:
$$p^+ + p^+ \rightarrow p^+ + \Sigma^+ + K^0$$
Underneath show the quarks in each particle.

b Use your answer to a to provide a quark analysis of what happens during the reaction.

CHAPTER 8

Completing the picture

By the end of this chapter you should be able to:

1 recall that electrons and neutrinos are members of a group of particles known as leptons, which are not affected by the strong force;

2 recall that protons, though more stable than other hadrons, are not completely stable but decay with a half-life that is thought to be of the order of 10^{32} years;

3 recall that there is a weak interaction between quarks and that this is responsible for beta (β) decay;

4 recall that there are two types of β-decay, involving the emission of either β⁻-particles (electrons) or β⁺-particles (antielectrons or positrons);

5 predict, from a graph showing neutron : proton ratios within nuclei, whether a decay is likely to result in a β⁻-particle or a β⁺-particle;

6 describe the two types of β-decay in terms of a simple quark model;

7 recall that (electron) neutrinos and (electron) antineutrinos are also produced during β⁺-decays and β⁻-decays respectively.

Leptons

As well as two types of hadron – particles which are affected by the *strong* force – there is another family of subatomic particles called **leptons**. Leptons are not affected by the strong force.

Scientists once thought that hadrons such as the protons and neutrons that we find in ordinary matter were fundamental particles. Further research showed that this was not so: hadrons are themselves made of smaller particles called quarks and their antiquark partners.

Fortunately for particle physicists, however, the story of leptons is much simpler than the story of hadrons that you met in chapters 4 and 7. Leptons, such as the **electron** that we find in all atoms, do not appear to be made of anything simpler. They really do seem to be fundamental particles.

But that isn't quite the end of the story. Just as there seem to be six different flavours of quark, so there also seem to be six different types of lepton, each with its corresponding antimatter particle.

Charged leptons

The first lepton to be discovered – in fact, the first subatomic particle to be discovered – was the electron (e⁻), in 1897. Then, in 1932, the antimatter partner of the electron, the **positron** (e⁺), was discovered. This was quickly followed by the discovery, in 1937, of a more massive 'heavy electron' called the **muon** or **mu-minus** particle (μ⁻). Much later, in 1975, a 'superheavy' electron, the **tau-minus** (τ⁻), was also discovered. Both the muon and the tau-minus particle have corresponding antimatter particles with the same mass but with the opposite electrical charge. The rest energies of these leptons are given in *box 8A*.

Box 8A The rest energies of some leptons		
electron	e⁻	5.11×10^{-4} GeV
mu-minus	μ⁻	1.06×10^{-1} GeV
tau-minus	τ⁻	1.78 GeV

SAQ 8.1

a What is the rest energy of a mu-plus particle?

b How many times more massive than an electron is:

(i) a muon;   (ii) a tau-minus particle?

Neutral leptons

The three leptons we have considered so far have all had a negative electrical charge and their antilepton partners all had a positive charge. There are three further members of the lepton family, plus the three corresponding antileptons, all of which are electrically neutral. These particles are called **neutrinos** ('tiny neutral ones') and antineutrinos respectively.

The existence of the first of these neutral leptons, the electron neutrino (ν_e), was predicted by Wolfgang Pauli in 1932. Physicists at that time were concerned that they could not explain measurements made during radioactive decays which emitted β-particles, i.e. electrons (*box 8B*).

Each electron emitted results from the decay of a neutron in the unstable nucleus of an atom:

$$n^0 \rightarrow p^+ + e^-$$

The emitted electrons were all expected to have the same amount of kinetic energy but careful measurements showed that their kinetic energy varied from zero to the amount of energy that was expected from the loss of mass during the decay. (This is unlike α-decay. All α-particles emitted by a particular radionuclide have the same energy.)

Pauli realised that the most likely explanation was that another particle was also emitted during this decay. Since this particle had never been detected, and it is electrically neutral particles that don't show up in detectors such as bubble chambers, Pauli decided that the new particle must be electrically neutral. Furthermore, the amount of energy involved meant that the particle must have very little rest mass/energy and perhaps none at all. So Pauli came up with the idea of the neutrino. (When the difference between matter and antimatter was better understood, scientists realised that the particle emitted during this decay is, in fact, an electron *antineutrino*.)

The complete equation for the β-decay is, therefore:

$$n^0 \rightarrow p^+ + e^- + \bar{\nu}_e$$

There are also neutrinos and antineutrinos corresponding to muons and tau leptons.

Having no electrical charge and little or no mass means that neutrinos are very difficult to detect and they were not observed until the mid-1950s. By then nuclear reactors were available which were able to produce billions of neutrinos each second. This meant that there was a reasonable chance of observing the occasional one interacting with matter. The Sun is a huge nuclear fusion reactor and billions of neutrinos from the Sun are, in fact, reaching your body every second. Almost all of these neutrinos pass straight through your body, and through the Earth itself, without interacting in any way (*box 8C on page 75*).

SAQ 8.2

a How accurate is the physics in John Updike's poem (see *box 8C*)?

b Where, on Earth, are the lover and his lass? Explain your answer.

Box 8C Wonderful neutrinos

Almost all of the neutrinos from the Sun which reach the Earth go straight through and out the other side. So neutrinos which strike the Earth in Nepal *at noon* come out on the other side of the Earth in … (where?).

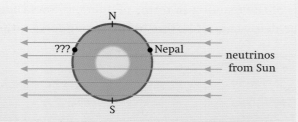

After seeing physicists drooling over the remarkable properties of neutrinos John Updike wrote a poem:

Cosmic Gall

Neutrinos they are very small.
They have no charge and have no mass
And do not interact at all,
The Earth is just a silly ball
To them, through which they simply pass,
At night they enter in Nepal
And pierce the lover and his lass
From underneath the bed – you call
It wonderful; I call it crass.

SAQ 8.3

The decay of a free neutron is the same as in a β–decay. Using the rest energy of all the other particles involved in the reaction*, calculate the maximum total energy (i.e. rest energy + kinetic energy) of an antineutrino emitted when a free neutron decays.

[* You will find these in *boxes 8A* and *8D*]

Summary of fundamental particles

At the time of writing (September 2000), physicists believe there are two pleasingly symmetrical sets of fundamental particles – quarks and leptons – plus two parallel sets of antiparticles. Each set contains just six particles (*figure 8.1*).

A fourth fundamental force

Not only do scientists want to know which *particles* are fundamental; they also want to know which *fundamental forces* affect the ways that these particles interact.

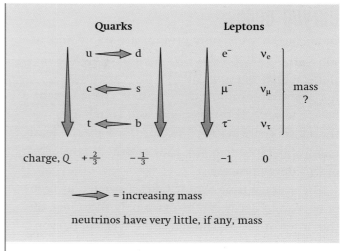

● **Figure 8.1** The fundamental particles.

Of the three fundamental forces mentioned in chapter 4:

■ The **gravitational force** is a very weak force but can act at long range. It has a significant effect only on large amounts of bulk matter and is not important at the level of individual particles.

■ The **electromagnetic force** can also act at long range. It holds electrons in atoms and is responsible for chemical bonds between atoms. It is also responsible for those particle decays or annihilations which involve the emission of γ-ray photons.

■ A **strong force**, which acts only at short range, is responsible for the reactions between colliding hadrons and for many hadron decays. The strong force *between* hadrons is the 'spillover' of the forces between quarks *inside* hadrons. Leptons are not affected by the strong force.

These three forces, however, are not the only fundamental forces. There are some particle decays which can only be explained if a fourth fundamental force called the **weak force** also exists.

Box 8D The rest energies of some baryons		
omega–minus	Ω^-	1.679 GeV
delta	$\Delta^-, \Delta^0, \Delta^+$	1.232 GeV
sigma–minus	Σ^-	1.197 GeV
sigma–zero	Σ^0	1.192 GeV
sigma–plus	Σ^+	1.189 GeV
lambda	Λ	1.116 GeV
neutron	n	0.9396 GeV
proton	p	0.9383 GeV

Baryon decays

Of all the baryons, only protons are stable and, as we shall see later, even they are not *completely* stable. Other baryons, all of which are more massive than protons, decay into baryons which have a lower rest mass/energy and which are, therefore, more stable. Since protons are the least massive baryons (*box 8D*), they are the final stage of this decay process.

The average time that it takes a particular type of baryon to decay can be extremely short, e.g. of the order of 10^{-23} s, though some types of baryon decay more slowly, e.g. in some cases in about 10^{-18} s or, in other cases, about 10^{-8} s. Neutrons survive much longer still before they decay, e.g. an average of 15 minutes for a free neutron and up to millions of years in some unstable (radioactive) nuclei with a long half-life. In stable nuclei neutrons can survive indefinitely.

Rapid (10^{-23} s) decays are due to **strong interactions**, i.e. to the action of the strong force between the quarks within a baryon. For example:

$$\Delta^+ \to p^+ + \pi^0$$
$$\Delta^0 \to p^+ + \pi^-$$

SAQ 8.4

a Using the information in *box 7E* on page 68, do a quark analysis of the decays of a Δ^+-particle and a Δ^0-particle. Then use your analysis to explain what happens during these decays.

b Compare the rest energy of each Δ-particle with the rest energies of the particles it decays into. Comment on your figures.

[The mesons π^0 and π^- have rest energies of 0.135 and 0.140 GeV respectively.]

The slightly less rapid (10^{-18} s) baryon decays are due to the electromagnetic force. For example:

$$\Delta^+ \to p^+ + \gamma$$

SAQ 8.5

Less than 1% of Δ^+-particles decay into a proton and a γ-ray photon. Suggest how the other 99% of them decay.

The following baryon decay is an example of the type that takes around 10^{-8} s:

$$\Sigma^+ \to n^0 + \pi^+$$

This decay does not emit a γ-ray photon so it cannot be due to the electromagnetic force. An analysis of the reaction in terms of quarks shows that the decay cannot be due to the strong force either:

$$
\begin{array}{ccc}
\Sigma^+ \to & n^0 & + \pi^+ \\
u & u & u \\
u & d & \bar{d} \\
s & d &
\end{array}
$$

The decay of the Σ^+-particle involves:
- the creation of a quark+antiquark pair $\{d\,\bar{d}\}$;
- a strange quark changing its flavour to become a down quark;
- a re-shuffling of quarks between the baryon and newly created meson.

One of the rules of strong interactions, however, is that quark flavour is conserved. The creation of the $\{d\,\bar{d}\}$ pair satisfies this rule, but the change of flavour s → d does not.

For this change of flavour to occur *another* force must be acting. This is called the weak force or **weak interaction**.

Though quark flavour is *not* conserved during weak interactions, the other conservation rules – electrical charge and baryon number – still apply.

The Σ^+-particle is in fact the *lightest* baryon with the quark composition $\{u\,u\,s\}$. So the only way it could possibly achieve a smaller rest mass/energy, and so become more stable, is by one of its quarks changing its flavour into a less massive quark.

SAQ 8.6

Suggest a possible reason why it is not one of the *up* quarks that changes its flavour during the decay of a Σ^+-particle.

SAQ 8.7

Using the information in *box 7E* on page 68, make a quark analysis of the following decay. Then use it to explain what happens during the decay:

$$\Sigma^+ \to p^+ + \pi^0$$

[Use $\{u\bar{u}\}$ for the π^0 particle.]

The weak interaction can change quarks between any pair of flavours, though the most frequent changes are:

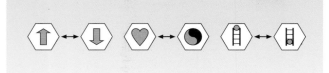

Leptons are also affected by the weak force, but only the following changes occur:

$$e^- \longleftrightarrow \nu_e \qquad \mu^- \longleftrightarrow \nu_\mu \qquad \tau^- \longleftrightarrow \nu_\tau$$

Beta decay

Beta (β) particles are one of the three types of radiation that can be emitted during the radioactive decay of an unstable nucleus of an atom (see *box 8B* on page 74). For example:

$$^{15}_{6}C \rightarrow {}^{15}_{7}N + {}^{0}_{-1}e$$

A neutron in the nucleus of the carbon atom has decayed into a proton and an electron (β-particle):

$$n^0 \rightarrow p^+ + e^-$$

As we saw earlier in this chapter, however, an electron antineutrino is also emitted:

$$n^0 \rightarrow p^+ + e^- + \bar{\nu}_e$$

To understand what is happening in this reaction, we need to show the quarks inside the neutron and proton:

$$
\begin{array}{ccc}
n^0 & \rightarrow & p^+ + e^- + \bar{\nu}_e \\
u & & u \\
d & & u \\
d & & d
\end{array}
$$

During the reaction, a down quark has changed its flavour to an up quark. This means that β-decay is caused by the weak force.

SAQ 8.8

a Using the information in *boxes 8A* and *8D* on pages 73 and 75 calculate the reduction in rest energy when a neutron decays to a proton.

b Why do you think that this reaction is so slow?

Two types of beta decay

In 1934, Irene Joliot-Curie and her husband made a previously unknown radioactive form (radioisotope) of phosphorus by bombarding aluminium with α-particles. They found that when this radioisotope decayed it emitted particles which behaved just like β-particles except that they had a *positive* electrical charge: they were **positrons**.

$$^{30}_{15}P \rightarrow {}^{30}_{14}Si + {}^{0}_{1}e$$

The complete particle equation for this reaction is:

$$
\begin{array}{ccc}
p & \rightarrow & n + e^+ + \nu_e \\
u & & u \\
u & & d \\
d & & d
\end{array}
$$

So there are, in fact, *two* types of β-decay:
- β⁻-decay, in which electrons (e⁻) are emitted;
- β⁺-decay, in which positrons (e⁺) are emitted.

$$\text{neutron} \underset{\beta^+}{\overset{\beta^-}{\rightleftharpoons}} \text{proton}$$

SAQ 8.9

Identify as many differences as you can between β⁻-decays and β⁺-decays.

Why there are two types of beta decay

A β⁺-decay seems to involve an *increase* of rest energy/mass so it shouldn't happen at all. The reason that it can sometimes happen is that the mass of a nucleus isn't simply the total mass of all the protons and neutrons it contains. It is always *less* than this by an amount which depends on the binding energy of the particular nucleus.

The graph in *figure 8.2* shows the masses of several different atoms all of which have 101 nucleons (protons and neutrons) but in different proportions.

You will notice that there is one particular combination of protons and neutrons which gives a nucleus with the least mass. This nucleus has the greatest value for the binding energy per nucleon and is, therefore, the most stable. All of the other atoms shown on the graph have nuclei which are less stable. These atoms will therefore decay in a way that makes them more stable: they will slide down the mass parabola one step at a time until they reach the lowest point.

Nuclei which are **proton-rich**, i.e. which have more protons than the most stable atom, will become more stable if protons change into neutrons. Nuclei which are **neutron-rich** will become more stable if neutrons change into protons. In other words:

- proton-rich nuclei become more stable by β^+-decays;
- neutron-rich nuclei become more stable by β^--decays.

SAQ 8.10

Use information from *figure 8.2* to describe, step by step, how each of the following atomic nuclei decays until it becomes stable:

a $^{101}_{47}Ag$ **b** $^{101}_{42}Mo$

Proton decay

The existence of β^+-decay shows that protons inside an unstable nucleus are themselves unstable. Protons inside stable nuclei and completely free protons seem to be very stable indeed. They are probably not, however, *completely* stable.

Physicists working on the detailed theory of particle physics have shown that at very high particle energies – of the order of 10^{15} GeV – it is theoretically possible for quarks to decay into leptons. A proton could, therefore, decay as shown:

$$p^+ \rightarrow \pi^0 + e^+$$
$$\begin{array}{cc} u & u \\ u & \bar{u} \\ d & \end{array}$$

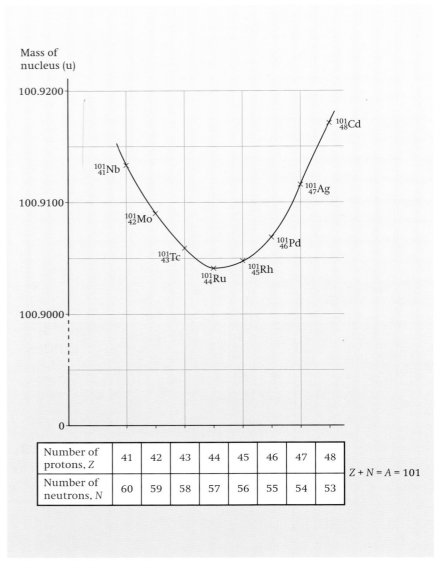

● **Figure 8.2** Mass parabola for mass (nucleon) number $A = 101$.

Number of protons, Z	41	42	43	44	45	46	47	48
Number of neutrons, N	60	59	58	57	56	55	54	53

$Z + N = A = 101$

If this decay can happen at all, it should happen *very occasionally* even to protons with the low energies they have in ordinary matter. Physicists' theories suggest a half-life for the protons in ordinary matter of between 10^{31} and 10^{33} years.

A half-life of 10^{31} years means that there should be just one proton decay per day in a 8000 m³ tank of water. Several experiments on this scale have been set up to detect such proton decays but none have so far been detected. This negative result has been interpreted as meaning that the half-life of 'free' protons (protons which are not held by the strong force to other protons or neutrons) is at least 10^{32} years.

SAQ 8.11

Explain why it is appropriate to look for the decay of 'free' protons using water molecules.

SAQ 8.12

The relationship between the mean kinetic energy of a population of particles and their temperature is given by:

$$E_k = \tfrac{3}{2}kT$$

where k is the Boltzmann constant (1.38×10^{-23} J K^{-1}) and T is the temperature (in kelvin).

To what temperature does a proton with a kinetic energy of 10^{15} GeV correspond?

Postscript

For completeness, two further matters should be briefly mentioned, even though they go beyond the requirements of A-level syllabuses.

Firstly, particle physicists believe that the four fundamental forces are themselves due to the effects of particles called **exchange particles**:
- **gravitons** in the case of gravitational forces;
- **photons** in the case of electromagnetic forces;
- **gluons** in the case of the strong force;
- **intermediate vector bosons** in the case of the weak force.

To date, all of the above particles, except for gravitons, have been detected.

Secondly, theory suggests that, at energies greater than about 10^{15} GeV, the strong, weak and electromagnetic forces are all the same strength and are, therefore, essentially the *same* force. Though such immensely high energies cannot be obtained inside particle accelerators or even inside stars, they probably did exist during the early seconds of the Universe. Paradoxically, particle physicists' understanding of the smallest things that are known has one of its most important applications in helping cosmologists to understand the largest thing that we know exists – the Universe itself (*figure 8.3*).

But that's another story.

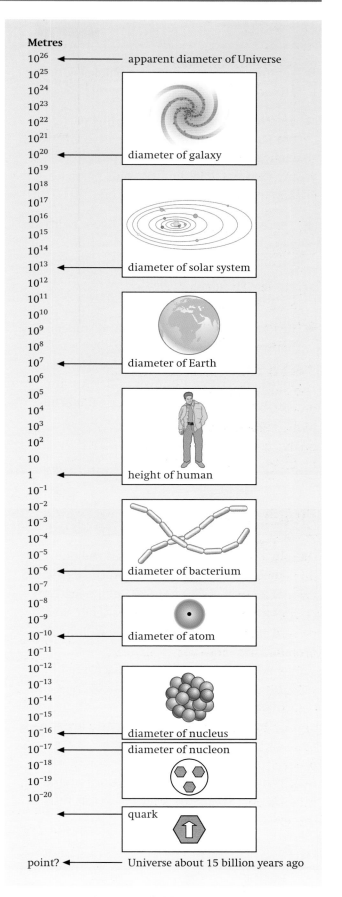

● **Figure 8.3** The scale of things.

SUMMARY

◆ Leptons are fundamental particles which are not affected by the strong force.

◆ Electrons, muons and tau-minus particles are leptons which have a negative electrical charge; their antiparticles – positrons, mu-plus particles and tau-plus particles – have a positive electrical charge.

◆ There is a neutral particle called a neutrino associated with each charged lepton; because these particles have no electrical charge, and have little or no mass, they hardly interact at all with matter.

◆ Reactions between hadrons and some hadron decays are due to the strong force. Other hadron decays involve quarks changing their flavour. Changes of flavour are due to another fundamental force called the weak force (or weak interaction).

◆ When some unstable atomic nuclei decay, they emit β-particles; this can be either a β⁻-particle (an electron) or a β⁺-particle (a positron).

◆ During β⁺-decay:
$$p^+ \rightarrow n^0 + e^+ + \nu_e \text{ (electron neutrino)}$$

◆ During β⁻-decay:
$$n^0 \rightarrow p^+ + e^- + \bar{\nu}_e \text{ (electron antineutrino)}$$

◆ Which type of β-decay occurs depends on whether a nucleus has less mass, and is more stable, by having fewer protons and more neutrons, or vice versa.

◆ Protons are the least massive type of baryon, so 'free' protons and protons in stable nuclei do not decay by strong or weak interactions. Protons are, however, probably not completely stable: scientists think that free protons have a half-life of the order of 10^{32} years.

Questions

1 In 1962, before he developed the quark theory, Gell-Mann predicted the existence of a fairly massive (1.680 GeV), negatively charged particle with a strangeness value of −3. He called this particle Ω^- (omega-minus).

When this particle was discovered in 1964 it was found to have an average life of about 8×10^{-11} seconds.

One of the ways that the particle decays is:

$$\Omega^- \rightarrow \Lambda^0 + K^-$$

What type of force (interaction) causes this decay? Justify your answer as fully as you can.

2 a Use the information below to draw a 'mass parabola' graph similar to *figure 8.2*.

   b Indicate on your graph:
      (i) the stable nucleus;
      (ii) the nuclei which undergo β⁻-decay;
      (iii) the nuclei which undergo β⁺-decay.

Symbol	Proton number, Z	Mass (u)
Sn	50	124.9708
Sb	51	124.9502
Te	52	124.9044
I	53	124.9046
Xe	54	124.9064

All the nuclei have a nucleon number (A) of 125.

Appendix

Hadrons

Baryon		Rest mass/energy		Quark composition	Life
proton	p$^+$	1.0073 u	0.9383 GeV	{u u d}	*Protons:*
neutron	n^0	1.0086 u	0.9396 GeV	{u d d}	half-life of at
lambda	L		1.116 GeV	{u d s}	least 10^{32}
sigma plus	Σ$^+$		1.189 GeV	{u u s}	years*.
sigma zero	Σ^0		1.192 GeV	{u d s}	*Neutrons:*
sigma minus	Σ$^-$		1.192 GeV	{d d s}	stable in
delta plus	Δ$^+$		1.232 GeV	{u u d}	stable nuclei*
delta zero	Δ^0		1.232 GeV	{u d d}	Half-life 15
delta minus	Δ$^-$		1.232 GeV	{d d d}	mins if free.
omega minus	Ω$^-$		1.679 GeV	{s s s}	*Others* exist
[1 u = 931.5 MeV		1 MeV = 10^6 eV		1 GeV = 10^9 eV]	for <10^{-10} s

[* in <u>un</u>stable nuclei, both protons and neutrons may decay (with half-lives that vary greatly)]

Meson		Rest mass/energy	Quark composition	Life
pi plus	π$^+$	0.134 GeV	{u d̄}	
pi zero	π^0	0.135 GeV	{u ū} or {d d̄}	
pi minus	π$^-$	0.134 GeV	{d ū}	all very
kay/kappa plus	K$^+$	0.494 GeV	{u s̄}	short-lived
kay/kappa zero	K^0	0.498 GeV	{d s̄}	[<10^{-10} s]
kay/kappa minus	K$^-$	0.494 GeV	{s ū}	
phi	φ	1.020 GeV	{s s̄}	
jay/psi	J/ψ	3.1 GeV	{c c̄}	

Leptons

Lepton		Rest mass/energy		Life
electron	e$^-$	0.005 u	5.11 × 10^{-4} GeV*	stable
muon/mu minus	μ$^-$		1.06 × 10^{-1} GeV	2 × 10^{-6} s
tauon/tau minus	τ$^-$		1.78 GeV	3.4 × 10^{-12} s
electron neutrino	ν$_e$	All with zero charge		
muon neutrino	ν$_μ$	All with very little, if any,		All stable
tauon neutrino	ν$_τ$	mass		
		[* i.e. 0.511 MeV]		

Quarks

Quark*		Charge	Baryon number	Strangeness
up	u	+ 2/3	+ 1/3	0
down	d	− 1/3	+ 1/3	0
strange	s	− 1/3	+ 1/3	−1

[* The quarks charm (c), bottom (b) and top (t) are also known to exist.]

[Note   The <u>unit</u> of electrical charge used here is that on an electron i.e. 1.602 × 10^{-19} C(oulomb). The direction of this charge on a particular hadron or lepton is indicated via a superscripted + or − beside the symbol for each particle. A superscripted zero or the absence of a superscript indicates no charge]

Anti-particles

An anti-particle has the same mass as the corresponding particle but the opposite charge and, where applicable, the opposite baryon number and strangeness. For example an anti-proton (p̄ or p$^-$) comprises {ū ū d̄} and has a charge of −1 and a baryon number of −1 but has zero strangeness like a proton.

Answers to questions

Chapter 1

1.1 $\dfrac{\text{diameter of nucleus}}{\text{diameter of atom}} = \dfrac{4 \times 10^{-15}}{1 \times 10^{-10}}$

$= \dfrac{1}{25\,000}$

In other words, if an atom were 25 metres in diameter, the nucleus would be just 1 millimetre in diameter.

1.2 **a** $^{14}_{6}\text{C}$ and $^{12}_{6}\text{C}$ both have 6 protons (i.e. $Z = 6$).
b $^{14}_{6}\text{C}$ has 8 neutrons but $^{12}_{6}\text{C}$ has only 6.

1.3 Their chemical reactions depend on the electrons in the space around the nucleus. Since $^{14}_{6}\text{C}$ and $^{12}_{6}\text{C}$ both have 6 protons, they both have 6 electrons.

Radioactivity is a nuclear phenomenon. The two extra neutrons in $^{14}_{6}\text{C}$ must make the nucleus less stable.

1.4 **a** (i) An α-particle is a helium nucleus.
(ii) A β-particle is an electron.
b When carbon-14 undergoes β-decay, a neutron in the nucleus changes into a proton and an electron. The electron is ejected from the nucleus.

1.5 During the fission of uranium-235 a neutron is lost from the fission fragments, but these still have the same number of protons as the uranium atom.
$^{141}_{55}\text{Cs}$ has 55 protons, so the rubidium has $92 - 55 = 37$ protons and has $235 - 141 - 1 = 93$ nucleons. So it is $^{93}_{37}\text{Rb}$.

1.6 $^{2}_{1}\text{H} + {}^{2}_{1}\text{H} \rightarrow {}^{3}_{1}\text{H} + {}^{1}_{1}\text{H}$ (or $^{1}_{1}\text{p}$)

1.7 **a** ΔE for $1\,\text{kg} = \Delta m\,c^2$
$= (2.998 \times 10^8)^2$
$= 8.988 \times 10^{16}\,\text{J}$
b 1.799×10^9 times as much, or about 1.8 billion times as much
c $1\,\text{u} = \dfrac{1.673 \times 10^{-27}}{1.0073}\,\text{kg}$
Multiplying this by $8.988 \times 10^{16}\,\text{J}$ gives:
ΔE for $1\,\text{u} = 1.49 \times 10^{-10}\,\text{J}$
d Dividing by 1.602×10^{-19} gives:
ΔE for $1\,\text{u} = 0.932 \times 10^9\,\text{eV}$
e $932 \times 10^6\,\text{eV} = 932\,\text{MeV}$
f In very round figures $1\,\text{u} = 1000\,\text{MeV}$

1.8 $^{232}\text{Th} \rightarrow {}^{228}\text{Ra} + \alpha$
$4.08\,\text{MeV} = \dfrac{4.08}{931.5}\,\text{u}$
So loss of mass $= 0.004\,\text{u}$
So mass of radium nucleus is:
$232.038 - 4.003 - 0.004 = 228.031\,\text{u}$

1.9 **a** A deuterium nucleus has 1 proton + 1 neutron.
A tritium nucleus has 1 proton + 2 neutrons.
b Neutrons have no electrical charge and therefore do not repel the proton or each other.

1.10 The centres of adjacent nucleons will be twice their radius (i.e. their diameter) apart. See *figure*.

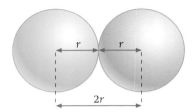

1.11 **a**

A	50	100	200
r (fm)	3.6	4.4	5.3

b When A doubles, r increases but by far less than double.

1.12 A nucleus without any nucleons has zero mass, so the graph line *must* go through the origin (0, 0). The line is, therefore, the one *through the origin* which best fits the plotted points.

1.13 **a** density $= \dfrac{3m}{4\pi r^3}$
$= \dfrac{3 \times 1.67 \times 10^{-27}}{4 \times 3.142 \times (1 \times 10^{-15})^3}$
$= 3.99 \times 10^{17}\,\text{kg m}^{-3}$
b, c This is much greater than the density of solids on Earth because atoms are mostly empty space in which electrons move around, with the nucleus taking up only a tiny fraction of the volume. In neutron stars, these electrons combine with protons in the nucleus to form neutrons so the star comprises only nuclear matter and has a similar density to nucleons. (Note: Using the round figure of 1 fm for nucleon radius is a little low, so the density calculation gives a high figure.)

1.14 **a** For two protons whose centres are 2 fm apart, the Coulomb force is:
$\dfrac{(1.602 \times 10^{-19})^2}{4 \times 3.142 \times 8.85 \times 10^{-12} \times (2 \times 10^{-15})^2} = 57.7\,\text{N}$
b At the same distance the gravitational force of attraction is:
$\dfrac{6.673 \times 10^{-11} \times (1.673 \times 10^{-27})^2}{(2 \times 10^{-15})^2} = 4.67 \times 10^{-35}\,\text{N}$
c The Coulomb force is 1.24×10^{36} times bigger than the gravitational force.

1.15 The red point indicates where the strong force of attraction and the Coulomb force of repulsion exactly balance each other.

The green part of the graph shows that if the protons are more than 2 fm apart, the strong force increases at first but then very quickly falls to zero.

The yellow part of the graph shows that if the distance between the centres of the protons falls very much below 2 fm, the strong force becomes a repulsive force.

1.16 **a, b** See *figure*.

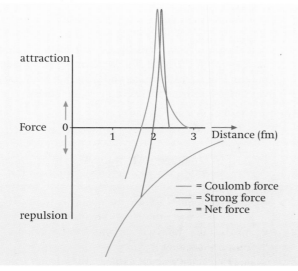

c (i) At less than 2 fm separation, the net force is repulsive.
(ii) At 2 fm separation, the forces are in balance.
(iii) At just over 2 fm, the net force is attractive.
(iv) At well over 2 fm the net force is repulsive.

1.17 **a, b**

Isotope	Neutrons	Neutron : proton ratio
$^{23}_{11}$Na	12	1.09
$^{24}_{12}$Mg	12	1.00
$^{40}_{20}$Ca	20	1.00
$^{56}_{26}$Fe	30	1.15
$^{107}_{47}$Ag	60	1.28
$^{208}_{82}$Pb	126	1.54

c The ratio is around 1 up to calcium-40 and then it becomes increasingly larger as the number of nucleons increases.

1.18 **b** (i) $N \approx Z$, on average, up to $Z = 8$
(ii) $N \approx Z$ for at least one isotope up to $Z = 20$
c Atoms with Z values between 83 and 92 are unstable. They are found in nature but are subject to spontaneous radioactive decay.

1.19 **a** Green = α-decay. N and Z are both too great and stability requires having fewer nucleons in nucleus.
Pink = β^--decay. N is too great for stability so a neutron changes to a proton.
Yellow = β^+-decay. Z is too great for stability so a proton changes to a neutron.
b Gamma radiation reduces the energy of a nucleus but has no effect on the number of protons and neutrons it contains.

1.20 **a** The loss of mass is:
$$\frac{2.1}{931.5} = 0.002\,25\,\text{u}$$

b proton + neutron   2.0159 u
less   0.0023 u
So mass of deuterium is   2.0136 u

1.21 **a** Iron-56 has the greatest binding energy per nucleon of any nucleus and is therefore energetically the most stable.
b Helium-4 and, to a lesser extent, carbon-12 and oxygen-16 all produce peaks on the graph of binding energy per nucleon and are, therefore, energetically more stable than one might expect for the number of nucleons they contain.
c To become more stable, smaller nuclei would have to become bigger (e.g. by joining together (fusing)) though not beyond iron-56.
d To become more stable, larger nuclei would have to split up, though not to less than iron-56.

End-of-chapter questions

1 **a** The graph should be the best fit *that goes through (0, 0)*.
b r_0 on this graph is about 1.25 fm.
c This value is 25% larger than the value obtained from the electron scattering graph (*figure 1.3*).

2 **a** The element with $Z = 50$, i.e. tin, has ten stable isotopes.
b $^{40}_{20}$Ca, $^{39}_{19}$K, $^{38}_{18}$Ar, $^{37}_{17}$Cl and $^{36}_{16}$S all have 20 neutrons.

3 The potential energy graph is the inverse of the binding energy graph (see *figure* below).

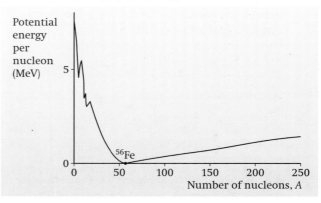

● Answer for question 3.

Chapter 2

2.1 $^{92}_{36}$Kr $\xrightarrow{\beta^-}$ $^{92}_{37}$Rb $\xrightarrow{\beta^-}$ $^{92}_{38}$Sr $\xrightarrow{\beta^-}$ $^{92}_{39}$Y $\xrightarrow{\beta^-}$ $^{92}_{40}$Zr

2.2 **a** There is $200/5 = 40$ times more energy released during fission of uranium-235 than during α-decay.
b $200\,\text{MeV} = 200 \times 10^6 \times 1.602 \times 10^{-19}\,\text{J}$
$= 3.204 \times 10^{-11}\,\text{J}$
Dividing this by 6.5×10^{-19} gives 5×10^7, i.e. 50 million times more.

2.3 **a**   92.92   235.04
     + 140.92   − 234.85
     +   1.01   0.19   u = loss in mass
     234.85
b $0.19\,\text{u} \times 931.5 = 177\,\text{MeV}$

2.4 We have:

^{93}Rb	8.6 MeV × 93	799.8
^{141}Cs	8.3 MeV × 141	1170.3
		1970.1
^{235}U	7.4 MeV × 235	1739.0
		231.1 MeV

This is roughly comparable to the figure obtained from mass calculation, but estimation from the graph is inevitably very much less accurate.

2.5 **a** Two neutrons are released, leaving 233 nucleons to be split 117 + 116. The graph in *figure 2.5* shows a 0.01% chance of this.

b Half of 235 is about 117. Since the total mass of the fragments must equal 235, for every nucleus with x nucleons *less* than 117 there will be another nucleus with x nucleons *more* than 117. So the graph below 117 will be the mirror image of the graph above 117. The image is not quite exact because of slight variability in nucleons emitted.

c The changes in mass/energy could be slightly greater for unequal splits.

2.6 $^4_2\text{He} + ^9_4\text{Be} \rightarrow ^{12}_6\text{C} + ^1_0\text{n}$

2.7 $\dfrac{10^{16}}{4.5 \times 10^9} = 2.2 \times 10^6$

The natural fission of uranium-238 is 2.2 million times less likely than α-decay.

2.8

Cube side (cm)	Neutrons produced ($10^6\,\text{s}^{-1}$)	Neutrons lost ($10^6\,\text{s}^{-1}$)	Sustainable? (Yes or No)
1	10	24	No
2	80	96	No [not quite]
3	270	216	Yes

A cube with each side between 2 and 3 cm would allow sustained fission. [In fact, the cube would need to have each side just greater than 2.4 cm. You should confirm this.]

2.9 A large piece of uranium implies loss of neutrons small enough to be ignored. Natural uranium is 99.3% uranium-238.

As the energy of fast neutrons falls because of repeated collisions, the neutrons are likely to be captured by uranium-238 (→ uranium-239 which decays to plutonium-239) before their energy falls low enough to be likely to cause fission of uranium-235.

2.10 For 400 K (127 °C, i.e. hot enough to raise steam):
kinetic energy $= \frac{3}{2} \times 1.38 \times 10^{-23} \times 400$
$= 8.28 \times 10^{-21}$ J
Dividing this by 1.602×10^{-19} gives 5.17×10^{-2} eV, i.e. 0.052 eV.

2.11 A single fission event releases an average of 2.5 neutrons. For sustained fission, one of these must cause further fission.

$\dfrac{1}{2.5} \times 100 = 40\%$

2.12 For every 1000 thermal neutrons that produce fission of uranium-235 atoms, 2500 fast neutrons are released. Around 1500 of these are captured during collisions with nuclei of uranium-238 or of moderator atoms and a few escape from the reactor. Around 1005 less energetic (thermal) neutrons remain. Control rods are adjusted to absorb just 5 of these thermal neutrons so that exactly 1000 are available to cause further fission, i.e. the reactor is critical. The fact that the 995 prompt neutrons are just subcritical and criticality is achieved via delayed neutrons makes this control feasible.

2.13 **a** A PWR uses water as a coolant.
Gas-cooled reactors use carbon dioxide as a coolant.

b In a PWR, water also acts as the moderator.
In gas-cooled reactors, carbon (graphite) is the moderator.

c In a PWR, water captures too many neutrons to be able to achieve criticality with natural uranium. So enriched uranium, with around 3% of uranium-235, is used as the fuel.
In a gas-cooled reactor, natural uranium (0.7% uranium-235) can be used as the fuel.

2.14 **a** With a small lump, neutrons escape from the lump faster than they are released by fission so the reaction cannot be sustained.

b Uranium-235 is not spontaneously fissile so, even with a lump which has greater than the critical mass, a source of neutrons is needed to start the reaction off. Once started, the reaction will then be sustained.

2.15 The fast neutrons emitted from the fission of plutonium-239 are effective in causing the fission of further plutonium-239 nuclei.

End-of-chapter questions

1 **a** There could be less uranium-235 in the samples from Oklo because, 2 billion years ago, there would have been >3% of uranium-235 in natural uranium. This uranium, together with groundwater as a moderator, could have produced a natural thermal fission reactor. This theory is supported by the fact that the percentages of neodymium isotopes at Oklo are much closer to those that result from uranium-235 fission than they are to the percentages found in samples of neodymium found elsewhere on Earth.

b This theory would be supported if some explanation were available of the source of neutrons to start the reaction.

2 Thermal neutrons have almost a thousand times greater chance of causing fission of uranium-235 nuclei than do fast neutrons.

Fast neutrons have rather less chance of causing fission of uranium-238 nuclei than they do with uranium-235 (and have hardly any chance at all of so doing once their energy falls below about 0.8 MeV). The chance of neutrons causing fission of uranium-238 nuclei, however, increases as their energy rises to 10 MeV, and above.

Chapter 3

3.1 The energy released per nucleon (and hence per unit mass) is greater in the fusion of hydrogen than in the fission of uranium, as can be seen from the relative steepness of the graph in *figure 3.1*. However, uranium has very many more nucleons in its nucleus so that the energy released per nucleus is far greater in the case of uranium.

3.2 **a** (i) Kinetic energy / work done to fuse nuclei

$$= \frac{(1.6 \times 10^{-19})^2}{4\pi \, 8.85 \times 10^{-12} \times 2 \times 10^{-15}} = 1.15 \times 10^{-13}\,\text{J}$$

   (ii) Dividing by 1.6×10^{-19} gives 7.2×10^5 eV, i.e. 0.72 MeV.

b Kinetic energy $= \frac{3}{2}kT$

$$= \frac{3}{2} \times 1.38 \times 10^{-23} \times T$$
$$\approx 2 \times 10^{-23} \times T$$

So $1.15 \times 10^{-13} = 2 \times 10^{-23} \times T$

$T = (1.15/2) \times 10^{10}$

$= 5.5 \times 10^9$ K

[Note: This is far higher than the Sun whose core temperature is about 1.5×10^7 K. However, the above temperature is that at which particles, on average, have the required kinetic energy. Because of the way that the energies of particles are distributed, there will always be *some* particles with the required energy even at much lower temperatures. The Sun contains such a large number of hydrogen nuclei in total that, even if only a very small proportion of these have the required energy, the overall rate of fission will still be quite high.]

On Earth, it is possible to achieve a temperature of about 10^8 K, so that a rather higher proportion of hydrogen nuclei than in the Sun would have enough energy for fusion to occur.

3.3 $2 \times 1.2 = 2.4$ MeV

3.4 $(3 \times 2.5) - (2 \times 1.2) = 5.1$ MeV

3.5 $(4 \times 7.2) - (6 \times 2.5) = 13.8$ MeV

3.6 **a**
$$\begin{aligned} 2 \times 2.4 &= 4.8 \\ 2 \times 5.1 &= 10.2 \\ & \underline{13.8} \\ & 28.8 \end{aligned}$$

[Check: This agrees with $4 \times 7.2 = 28.8$.]

b (i) $\dfrac{28.8}{931.5} = 0.031$ u

   (ii) $\dfrac{0.031}{4 \times 1.0073} \times 100 = 0.77\%$

c Overall, hydrogen-1 nuclei are consumed by the process so it isn't really a cycle. However, of every six hydrogen-1 nuclei that take part in the series of reactions, two are recycled.

3.7 The rate of proton–proton fusion in the Sun is $5 \times 10^{-18} \times 10^{56}$, i.e. 5×10^{38} per second. [In fact, it is slightly less because not all the protons are in the Sun's core.]

3.8 **a** $4\,^1_1\text{H} \rightarrow \,^4_2\text{He} + 2\,^0_1\text{e} + 2\nu$

b The overall reaction is exactly the same as for the hydrogen cycle.

c The energy released will also be exactly the same as for the hydrogen cycle.

d The series of reactions is also called the CNO cycle because $^{12}_6\text{C} \rightarrow \,^{12}_6\text{C}$ via a series of isotopes of carbon, nitrogen and oxygen.

3.9 It is very unlikely that three nuclei will collide simultaneously, so this overall fusion is normally achieved via a series of two-particle fusion reactions.

3.10 Iron-56 is the nucleus with the maximum binding energy per nucleon and so is energetically the most stable.

3.11 The Sun is a third generation star because there was sufficient heavy elements in the material from which it was formed to produce planets.

3.12
$$\begin{aligned} \text{D has binding energy } 1.2\,\text{MeV} \times 2 &= 2.4 \\ \text{T has binding energy } 2.9\,\text{MeV} \times 3 &= \underline{8.7} \\ \text{Total binding energy} & 11.1 \\ \text{He has binding energy } 7.2\,\text{MeV} \times 4 &= 28.8 \\ & \underline{-\,11.1} \\ \text{Energy released by D–T fusion} & 17.7\,\text{MeV} \end{aligned}$$

3.13 **a** $^2_1\text{H} + \,^2_1\text{H} \rightarrow \,^3_2\text{He} + \,^1_0\text{n}$
   $^2_1\text{H} + \,^2_1\text{H} \rightarrow \,^3_1\text{H} + \,^1_1\text{H}$

b D has binding energy 1.2 MeV $\times 2 = 2.4$
   $\times 2 = 4.8$
   ^{3}He has binding energy 2.6 MeV $\times 3 = 7.8$
   The difference (energy released) is 3.0 MeV.
   D has binding energy 1.2 MeV $\times 2 = 2.4$
   $\times 2 = 4.8$
   T has binding energy 2.9 MeV $\times 3 = 8.7$
   The difference (energy released) is 3.9 MeV.

c $2\,^1_1\text{H} \rightarrow \,^2_1\text{H}$ fusion releases only 2×1.2 MeV $= 2.4$ MeV

3.14 Hydrogen-3 is tritium and so is used after extraction in the D–T fusion reaction itself.

3.15 If there are e.g. 100 000 turns on the primary coil and the charged particles in the plasma act as a single turn secondary coil, then the current in the secondary will be 100 000 times bigger than the current in the primary. So a current of e.g. 100 A in the primary will induce a current of 10 million A in the plasma.

End-of-chapter questions

1 **a** There is no Coulomb barrier to overcome when a neutron approaches a nucleus because the neutron has no electrical charge.

b A nucleus cannot capture very many neutrons before reaching a neutron : proton ratio that is unstable.

2 **a** Starting with carbon-12 → nitrogen-13:

Δm (u)	ΔE (MeV)
0.0021	1.96
0.0018*	1.68
0.0081	7.55
0.0078	7.27
0.0025*	2.33
0.0053	4.94

[* These figures take account of the rest mass of the positron formed in these reactions.]

b Total   25.73 MeV

3 Fusion would be environmentally very clean, producing no polluting gases (e.g. sulphur dioxide, nitrogen oxides, carbon dioxide) and very little radioactive waste with a long half-life. Some radioisotopes are formed in structures of the reactors but these can be reduced by careful choice of materials. It also has a virtually unlimited fuel supply. However, it is not yet technically achievable on a useful scale.

Fission is also environmentally clean so far as polluting gases are concerned, but it does produce radioactive waste with a long half-life and there are limited supplies of the nuclear fuel. Fast breeder reactors would reduce both these problems by converting uranium-238 (99.3% of natural uranium) into fissile plutonium-239 which is the fuel for the fast breeder reactor. However, fast breeder reactors are technically less well developed than thermal reactors and give rise to concerns because plutonium-239 is a weapons-grade fissile material.

Chapter 4

4.1 A truly fundamental particle cannot be split up into anything smaller so the word *atom* (= 'can't be cut') is a very appropriate term for one.

4.2 $\dfrac{\text{diameter of atomic nucleus}}{\text{diameter of atom}} \approx \dfrac{10^{-14}}{10^{-10}} \approx 10^{-4}$

So a nucleus is about 10^4 (10 000) times smaller in diameter than an atom.

4.3 **a** At distances of about the diameter of a nucleon:
■ the strong force is about 100 (10^2) times greater than the electromagnetic force;
■ the electromagnetic force is about 10^{36} times greater than the gravitational force.
So the strong force is about 10^{38} times greater than the gravitational force.

b The strong force plays no part in holding electrons to the nuclei of atoms because it only acts between nucleons.

[The electrons would, in any case, be much too far away from the nucleus to be affected by the strong force.]

The strong force does not hold atoms to each other because the nuclei of atoms are typically 10^{-10} m apart and the strong force does not act to any significant extent at distances greater than 10^{-14} m.

4.4 Antimatter particles have the same mass as their equivalent matter particles and the force of gravity between two particles is directly proportional to each of their masses.

4.5 A neutron does not have an electrical charge, so it is not possible for an antineutron to have the opposite electrical charge. (The difference between a neutron and an antineutron will be explained on page 68 when considering the even smaller particles that neutrons are, in fact, made of.)

4.6 **a** proton + neutron → proton + proton + pi-minus
b p^+ + n^0 → p^+ + p^+ + π^-

4.7 **a** $\Delta^- \to n^0 + \pi^-$
b $\Sigma^+ \to p^+ + \pi^0$

4.8 $K^0 \to \pi^+ + \pi^-$

End-of-chapter questions
1

Date	Particles thought to be fundamental
early 19th century	atoms
1890s to 1930s	electrons, protons and neutrons
by 1960s	other leptons besides electrons; + other hadrons besides protons and neutrons; + an antimatter particle for each matter particle.

2 If other leptons and hadrons were stable, there would be many more types of atoms and so many more different chemical compounds also.

Chapter 5

5.1 $\Delta E = \Delta m\, c^2$
$= 0.241 \times 10^{-27} \times (3 \times 10^8)^2$
$= 2.17 \times 10^{-11}$ J

5.2 n → p loss in mass of 0.002×10^{-27} kg
π^- gain in mass of 0.250×10^{-27} kg
Δm overall is a gain of 0.248×10^{-27} kg.
So overall loss of kinetic energy is:
$0.248 \times 10^{-27} \times (3 \times 10^8)^2 = 2.23 \times 10^{-11}$ J

5.3 $E = QV$
The charge on an electron is 1.602×10^{-19} C. So 1 electron-volt (eV), i.e. the energy transferred to an electron when it moves across a potential difference of 1 volt, is 1.602×10^{-19} J.

5.4 The rest energies of protons and neutrons are in proportion to mass:

$\dfrac{\text{mass of neutron}}{\text{mass of proton}} = \dfrac{1.675}{1.673}$

The rest energy of a neutron is
$\dfrac{1.675}{1.673} \times 0.938$ GeV, i.e. 0.939 GeV.

5.5 0.134 GeV

5.6 **a** 5.11×10^{-4} GeV = 0.511 MeV
b When e^+ and e^- annihilate each other, their rest energies and their kinetic energies are transferred as two γ-ray photons.

The total rest energies = 1.022 MeV so the total energy of the γ-ray photons must be 1.022 MeV plus whatever kinetic energy the two colliding particles had.

5.7 One-third the speed of light is 1×10^8 m s^{-1}. The distance travelled in 10^{-9} s is $10^8 \times 10^{-9}$ m, i.e. 10^{-1} m (or 10 cm).

5.8 Detecting particles using *scintillations in phosphors* isn't very sensitive. The phosphor is also on a 2-D surface so particles will be detected only if they *cross* the plane of this surface. The paths of particles will be shown only if they move *in* the plane of the phosphor surface.
Ionisation trails:
- on film have the same drawbacks as phosphors unless *thick* emulsion is used. This can then be cut into thin slices after processing to analyse the track inside the emulsion. Film does, however, produce a permanent record;
- in cloud chambers are 3-D so there is a far greater chance of detecting the paths of particles;
- bubble chambers have the advantages of cloud chambers plus they can give up to 30 readings per second;
- electronic detectors can take millions of readings per second all of which can be analysed by computer.

5.9 Assuming particles are travelling at one-tenth the speed of light, i.e. $3 \times 10^7 \, \mathrm{m\,s^{-1}}$:
  a 5 cm (0.05 m) represents $0.05 \div (3 \times 10^7) = 1.7 \times 10^{-9} \, \mathrm{s}$ (i.e. 1.7 nanoseconds).
  b 3 mm (0.003 m) represents $1 \times 10^{-10} \, \mathrm{s}$.

5.10 The conventional current (the direction of flow of *positive* charge) is up and the force changing the direction of the positron acts towards the left so, by Fleming's left-hand rule, the direction of the magnetic field is into the paper.

5.11 **a** The path of the positron is more curved after it has passed through the lead plate.
  b This is because the positron has lost kinetic energy due to collisions in the lead plate and is moving more slowly.

5.12 Trace B curves in the opposite direction, so it was produced by a particle with the opposite charge to a proton (i.e. by a negatively charged particle). Trace B is also far more curved so the mass of the particle is a lot less and/or its speed is a lot lower. (It could be an electron.) This particle is also losing energy at a proportionally greater rate as it spirals inwards.

End-of-chapter question

1 **a** See *figure*.

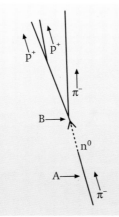

● Answer for question 1.

b The path of the neutron can be identified, even though it causes no ionisation, because it is created in collision A and it creates other detectable particles in collision B. So the path of the neutron is from A to B.
  The pi-zero particle that is also created in collision A does not produce ionisation and also does not create any further particles, so its path cannot be identified on the diagram.

c Collision A   rest energies (GeV):

π^-	0.134	n^0	0.939
p^+	0.938	π^0	0.135
	1.072		1.074

The rest energy increases by 0.002 GeV, so this amount of kinetic energy is lost.

Collision B		rest energies (GeV)	
n^0	0.939	p^+	0.938
(p^+)		(p^+)	
		π^-	0.134

The rest energy increases by 0.133 GeV, so this amount of kinetic energy is lost.

Chapter 6

6.1 Particle physics is also known as high-energy physics because new particles can only be produced by accelerating existing particles (e.g. protons or electrons) to very high speeds, i.e. giving them very high kinetic energies.

6.2 The TV tube is a 4000 eV (4 keV) electron accelerator.

6.3 The tubular electrodes are progressively longer because as the electrons are accelerated and move faster they travel further during each half cycle of the applied alternating voltage.

6.4 $f = \dfrac{Bq}{2\pi m}$

$$= \dfrac{8.95 \times 10^{-4} \times 1.602 \times 10^{-19}}{2 \times 3.142 \times 1.673 \times 10^{-27}}$$

$$= 1.36 \times 10^4 \, \mathrm{Hz}$$

6.5 The path of the proton in the bubble chamber is less curved than the path of the proton in the cyclotron. (This is because the magnetic field isn't so strong.)
  Also the spiral path in the cyclotron becomes less and less curved as the proton is accelerated whereas in the bubble chamber the path of the proton becomes slightly more curved as the proton loses kinetic energy through collisions.

6.6 $E_k = \frac{1}{2}mv^2$

$$1.602 \times 10^{-19} \times 25 \times 10^6 = \tfrac{1}{2}(1.673 \times 10^{-27})v^2$$

$$v^2 = \dfrac{2 \times 1.602 \times 25}{1.673} \times \dfrac{10^{-13}}{10^{-27}}$$

$$= 47.9 \times 10^{14}$$

$$v = 6.92 \times 10^7$$

$$\dfrac{v}{c} = \dfrac{6.92 \times 10^7}{3 \times 10^8} = 0.231$$

The proton moves at 0.231 (23.1%) of light speed.

6.7 The limiting velocity, which is approached more and more closely but never reached, is the speed of light.

6.8   **a** $E_k = mc^2 \left(\dfrac{1}{\sqrt{1 - \dfrac{v^2}{c^2}}} - 1 \right)$

   (i)   When $v = 0$:
   $$E_k = mc^2(\tfrac{1}{\sqrt{1}} - 1)$$
   $$= mc^2\,(0) = 0$$

   (ii)   When $v = c$:
   $$E_k = mc^2\,(\sqrt{\tfrac{1}{[1-1]}} - 1)$$
   $$= mc^2\,(\tfrac{1}{0} - 1)$$
   i.e. E_k is infinite (∞).

b   When v is small:
$$\frac{1}{\sqrt{1 - \dfrac{v^2}{c^2}}} \approx 1 + \frac{v^2}{2c^2}$$

$$E_k = mc^2\left(1 + \frac{v^2}{2c^2}\,1\right)$$
$$= \tfrac{1}{2}mc^2v^2/c^2 = \tfrac{1}{2}mv^2$$

(i.e. the usual [Newtonian] formula for kinetic energy).

6.9   The synchrotron is a cyclotron in which the frequency of the alternating potential difference changes so that the reversals in the direction of this alternating potential difference stay synchronised with the times when the particles are travelling through the acceleration cavities.

6.10 $v = \dfrac{Bqr}{m}$ (see *box 6B* on page 58)

So $v \propto r$

and $v \propto \dfrac{1}{m}$

   For the LEP r is larger and $\frac{q}{m}$ is much larger for electrons (and positrons) than it is for protons (and antiprotons).

   So the LEP accelerates particles to a much higher speed than the SPS.

   The SPS has a radius of 1.1 km. It accelerates protons and antiprotons to energies of 450 GeV.

   The LEP has a larger diameter so that it can accelerate particles to a higher speed than the SPS. However, the electrons (and positrons) it accelerates have a much smaller mass than protons (and anti-protons) so the LEP produces particles with less kinetic energy than the SPS.

6.11   For protons/antiprotons with mass m
initial $E_k = \tfrac{1}{2}mv^2$

   final $E_k = 2(\tfrac{1}{2}m\,[0.47v]^2) + \tfrac{1}{2}m\,[0.33v]^2$
   $$= 0.22\,mv^2 + 0.05\,mv^2$$
   $$= 0.27\,mv^2$$

$\dfrac{\text{final } E_k}{\text{initial } E_k} = \dfrac{0.27}{0.5} = 0.54$ (54%)

6.12   The CERN LEP accelerates electrons/positrons to energies of 50 GeV. So $e^- e^+$ collisions occur with an energy of 100 GeV.

   The Fermilab teratron accelerates protons/anti-protons to energies of 1000 GeV. So proton/antiproton collisions occur with an energy of 2000 GeV.

6.13   The chance of collision is in proportion to the number of particles in a 1 cm² cross-section.

   In a fixed target the number of particles is $10^{25}/10^{11} = 10^{14}$ times greater than in a beam. So the chance of collision is also 10^{14} times greater.

End-of-chapter questions

1   **a**   Rest energy of J/ψ = 3.1 GeV
Rest energy of proton = 0.938 GeV
So the rest energy/mass of J/ψ is 3.3 times greater than that of a proton.

b   The kinetic energy of the colliding electrons and positrons needed to produce a J/ψ particle would need to be at least half of 3.1 GeV, i.e. at least 1.55 GeV.

c   To create J/ψ particles, protons fired at a fixed target would need to have double the kinetic energy of colliding electrons/positrons, even if the same percentage of the kinetic energy was used to create new matter as in electron–positron collisions.

2   **a**   The largest particle accelerators have diameters of several kilometres (10^3 metres). Protons have a diameter of about 1 fm (10^{-15} metres). So the largest particle accelerators are 10^{18} times greater in diameter than protons (and even more times greater in diameter than electrons).

b   There are no correct answers to this question. Everyone should have their own answers, however, depending on their ethical and political points of view and the things that they consider to be most important in life.

Chapter 7

7.1   **a**   Protons and neutrons are baryons.
   b   Pions are mesons.

7.2 Δ^- and Σ^+ both decay to form a baryon plus a pion. Pions are mesons and baryon number is conserved, so Δ^- and Σ^+ must both be baryons.

7.3   **a**
$$\pi^- + p^+ \rightarrow K^+ + \Sigma^-$$
Q $(-1) + (+1)$ $(+1) + (-1)$
      total 0   total 0
B $0 + (+1)$ $0 + (+1)$
      total +1   total +1
Q and B both conserved $\therefore$ can happen

b
$$n^0 + p^+ \rightarrow n^0 + p^+ + p^+ + \pi^-$$
B $(+1) + (+1)$ $(+1) + (+1) + (+1) + 0$
      total +2   total +3
B not conserved $\therefore$ cannot happen

c
$$\Sigma^+ \rightarrow \Lambda + \pi^-$$
Q $+1$ $0 + (-1)$
Q not conserved $\therefore$ cannot happen

d
$$p^+ + p^+ \rightarrow \pi^- + p^+ + n^0$$
Q $(+1) + (+1)$ $(-1) + (+1) + 0$
      total $^+2$ total 0
Q not conserved $\therefore$ cannot happen

7.4 **a** $p^+ + p^+ \rightarrow p^+ + \Sigma^+ + \pi^0$

S $0 + 0 \qquad 0 + (-1) + 0$

total 0 total -1

S not conserved $\therefore$ cannot happen

b $p^+ + p^+ \rightarrow p^+ + \Sigma^+ + K^0$

Q $(+1) + (+1) \qquad (+1) + (+1) + 0$

total $+2$ total $+2$

B $(+1) + (+1) \qquad (+1) + (+1) + 0$

total $+2$ total $+2$

S $0 + 0 \qquad 0 + (-1) + (+1)$

total 0 total 0

Q, B and S all conserved $\therefore$ can happen

c (i) $K^+ + p^+ \rightarrow \pi^+ + \Sigma^+$

Q $(+1) + (+1) \quad (+1) + (+1)$ OK

B $0 + (+1) \quad 0 + (+1)$ OK

S $(+1) + 0 \quad 0 + (-1)$ X

S not conserved $\therefore$ cannot happen

(ii) $K^- + p^+ \rightarrow \pi^+ + \Sigma^-$

Q $(-1) + (+1) \quad (+1) + (-1)$ OK

B $0 + (+1) \quad 0 + (+1)$ OK

S $(+1) + 0 \quad 0 + (-1)$ X

S not conserved $\therefore$ cannot happen

7.5

Antiquark (flavour)	Charge (Q)	Baryon number (B)	Strangeness (S)
$\bar{u}$	$-\frac{2}{3}$	$-\frac{1}{3}$	0
$\bar{d}$	$+\frac{1}{3}$	$-\frac{1}{3}$	0
$\bar{s}$	$+\frac{1}{3}$	$-\frac{1}{3}$	$+1$

7.6 **a** $\{u \qquad d \qquad d\}$ Baryon X

Q $+\frac{2}{3} \quad -\frac{1}{3} \quad -\frac{1}{3} \rightarrow 0$

B $+\frac{1}{3} \quad +\frac{1}{3} \quad +\frac{1}{3} \rightarrow +1$

S $0 \qquad 0 \qquad 0 \rightarrow 0$

So baryon X has the properties of a neutron.

b $\{u \qquad \bar{s}\}$ Meson Y

Q $+\frac{2}{3} \quad +\frac{1}{3} \rightarrow +1$

B $+\frac{1}{3} \quad -\frac{1}{3} \rightarrow 0$

S $0 \qquad +1 \rightarrow +1$

So meson Y has the properties of a K$^+$-particle

7.7 An antineutron is $\{\bar{u} \quad \bar{d} \quad \bar{d}\}$.

Q $0 \qquad -\frac{2}{3} \quad +\frac{1}{3} \quad +\frac{1}{3}$

The antineutron, like the neutron, has no *overall* charge. The charges on its three antiquarks, however, are each the opposite of the charges on the corresponding quarks of a neutron.

7.8 $p^+ + p^+ \rightarrow p^+ + n^0 + \pi^+$

$u \quad u \quad u \quad u \quad u$

$u \quad u \quad u \quad d \quad \bar{d}$

$d \quad d \quad d \quad d$

a A $\{d \; \bar{d}\}$ quark+antiquark pair is created in this reaction.

b A $\{d \; \bar{d}\}$ quark+antiquark pair is a π^0 meson. The quarks in this meson and those in a proton have then rearranged to produce a neutron and a π^+ meson.

7.9 $\lambda = \dfrac{h}{mv}$

$= \dfrac{6.626 \times 10^{-34}}{9.1 \times 10^{-31} \times 0.3 \times 10^8}$

$= 2.4 \times 10^{-11}$ m

This is about 2×10^4 times shorter than the wavelength of light, but is still about 2×10^4 times greater than the diameter of a nucleon ($\cong 1$ fm). So to 'see' nucleons, or the quarks inside nucleons, electrons with even higher energies are needed. Calculations relating to these electrons must use relativistic formulae (see *box 6C* on page 58).

End-of-chapter questions

1 **a** $K^- + p^+ \rightarrow K^0 + K^+ + \Omega^-$

$s \quad u \quad d \quad u \quad s$

$\bar{u} \quad u \quad \bar{s} \quad \bar{s} \quad s$

$d \qquad\qquad\qquad\qquad s$

b Two strange quark+antiquark pairs have been created. These extra quarks were produced from the energy of the collision and the energy released by the annihilation of an already existing quark+anti-quark pair (see answer to **c**).

c An up quark+antiquark pair have disappeared. The up quark and antiquark have annihilated each other, their rest energy contributing to the creation of the two extra quark+antiquark pairs.

2 **a** $p^+ + p^+ \rightarrow p^+ + \Sigma^+ + K^0$

$u \quad u \quad u \quad u \quad d$

$u \quad u \quad u \quad u \quad \bar{s}$

$d \quad d \quad d \quad s$

b The reaction produces a strange quark+antiquark pair. These, together with the quarks in a proton, rearrange to produce the Σ^+-particle and K^0-particle.

Chapter 8

8.1 **a** A μ^+-particle has the same rest energy as a μ^--particle, i.e. 1.06×10^{-1} GeV.

b The rest energy of an electron is 5.11×10^{-4} GeV.

(i) So a muon is $\dfrac{1.06 \times 10^{-1}}{5.11 \times 10^{-4}}$ times more massive than an electron, i.e. 2.07×10^2 (207) times as massive.

(ii) A tau-minus particle is $\dfrac{1.78}{5.11 \times 10^{-4}}$ times more massive than an electron, i.e. 3.48×10^3 (3480) times as massive.

8.2 **a** Neutrinos are very small, with no charge and very little mass (or possibly no mass at all).

It is not true to say that they do not interact at all with other matter. The chances of interaction when a neutrino passes through a body as large and as dense as the Earth is, however, very small.

b The lover and his lass would be in Texas. Most neutrinos from the Sun which enter the Earth at noon in Nepal would pass right through the Earth and come out on the opposite side, i.e. in Texas, shortly after midnight and so pierce the lover and his lass from *underneath* the bed.

8.3

$$n^0 \rightarrow p^+ + e^- + \bar{v_e}$$

rest energies   0.9396   0.9383   0.0005
(GeV)   total 0.9388

There is a loss of rest energy of 0.0008 GeV. This is, therefore, the maximum total energy of the antineutrino, i.e. its kinetic energy plus its rest energy (if any).

8.4 **a** $\Delta^+ \rightarrow p^+ + \pi^0$

u   u   u
u   u $\bar{u}$
d   d

When a Δ^+-particle decays, some of its rest energy/mass creates an up quark+antiquark pair (a π^0 meson). A proton with the same quarks as a Δ^+-particle, but with a lower rest energy/mass, remains.

$\Delta^0 \rightarrow p^+ + \pi^-$
u   u   d
d   u $\bar{u}$
d   d

When a Δ^0-particle decays, some of its rest energy/mass creates an up quark+antiquark pair. These, together with the quarks from the Δ^0-particle, rearrange to create a proton and a π^--particle.

b Δ^+ $\rightarrow$ p^+ + π^0
rest energies   1.232   0.938   0.135
(GeV)   total   1.073
The lost 0.159 GeV of rest energy appears as kinetic energy of the particles produced by the decay.
                Δ^0 $\rightarrow$ p^+ + π^-
rest energies   1.232   0.938   0.140
(GeV)   total   1.078
The lost 0.154 GeV of rest energy appears as kinetic energy of the particles produced by the decay.

8.5 99% of Δ^+-particles in fact decay in the alternative way which is given on page 76, i.e. into a proton plus a neutral pion.

8.6 The reason an up quark does not change its flavour during the decay of a Σ^+-particle is that this would *increase* its rest energy/mass.

8.7 $\Sigma^+ \rightarrow p^+ + \pi^0$
u   u   u
u   u $\bar{u}$
s   d

A {u $\bar{u}$} quark+antiquark pair is created. The strange quark changes its flavour to become a down quark.

8.8 $n^0 \rightarrow$ p^+ + e^- $+ \bar{v}_e$
rest energies   0.9396   0.9383   0.0005
(GeV)
a The reduction in *baryon* rest energy as a result of this decay is 0.0008 GeV.

b This very small reduction in rest mass/energy means that the neutron is only slightly less stable than the proton. There is, therefore, only a very slight tendency for the decay to occur, which explains the relatively long half-life of a free neutron.

8.9

β⁺-decay	β⁻-decay
proton → neutron	neutron → proton
positron emitted	electron emitted
neutrino emitted	antineutrino emitted
u → d	d → u

8.10 **a** $^{101}_{47}\text{Ag} \xrightarrow{\beta^+} {}^{101}_{46}\text{Pd} \xrightarrow{\beta^+} {}^{101}_{45}\text{Rh} \xrightarrow{\beta^+} {}^{101}_{44}\text{Ru}$

      b $^{101}_{42}\text{Mo} \xrightarrow{\beta^-} {}^{101}_{43}\text{Tc} \xrightarrow{\beta^-} {}^{101}_{44}\text{Ru}$

8.11 The chemical bonding between hydrogen and oxygen atoms in water molecules is due to electrons in the space surrounding the nuclei of the atoms. The single proton in each hydrogen atom is still separated by many times its own diameter from other nucleons and is, therefore, free from interactions with them.

     Also we need a very large mass to provide enough protons to make a collision at all likely. So it is convenient that we can use a cheap and easily obtained substance such as water.

8.12 $10^{15}\,\text{GeV} = 10^{24}\,\text{eV}$
$$= 10^{24} \times 1.6 \times 10^{-19}\,\text{J}$$
$$= 1.6 \times 10^5\,\text{J}$$
$$E_k = \tfrac{3}{2}kT$$
$$1.6 \times 10^5 = \frac{3 \times 1.38 \times 10^{-23} \times T}{2}$$
$$\text{So} \quad T = \frac{2 \times 1.6 \times 10^5}{3 \times 1.38 \times 10^{-23}} = 7.73 \times 10^{27}\,\text{K}$$

End-of-chapter questions

1 $\Omega^- \rightarrow \Lambda^0 + K^-$
s   u   s
s   d $\bar{u}$
s   s

A {u $\bar{u}$} quark+antiquark pair is created.
An s quark changes into a d quark.
A rearrangement of quarks occurs.
     The change of flavour indicates that the decay is caused by the weak force (interaction). The life-span of the Ω^--particle (about 10^{-10} seconds) also suggests the weak interaction (typically 10^{-8} seconds) rather than the electromagnetic force (typically 10^{-18} seconds) or the strong force (typically 10^{-23} seconds).

2   **a** The graph should be in the same format as *figure 8.2*.
     b (i) $^{125}_{52}\text{Te}$ is the stable nucleus.
        (ii) $^{125}_{50}\text{Sn}$ and $^{125}_{51}\text{Sb}$ undergo β^--decay.
       (iii) $^{125}_{54}\text{Xe}$ and $^{125}_{53}\text{I}$ undergo β^+-decay.

Glossary of key terms and units

[*Note* Further information about asterisked items can be found in the appendix.]

anti-matter	comprises particles with the same mass as the corresponding particles of matter but with the opposite electrical charge (or, if neutral *baryons*, with oppositely charged *quarks*).
baryons*	*hadrons* comprising three *quarks*. *Protons* and *neutrons* are baryons found in ordinary matter.
binding energy	the loss in mass/energy when *nucleons* cluster together to form an atomic nucleus. This energy needs to be supplied to separate the nucleons; it can be thought of as the energy that binds them together.
Coulomb force	the force between two electrically charged bodies, sometimes referred to as the electrostatic or the electromagnetic force. It holds *electrons* in the space around the nucleus in an atom.
critical	a nuclear *fission* reaction that is producing just enough *neutrons* to keep going. Otherwise the reaction is subcritical and stops or supercritical and accelerates uncontrollably.
electron*	the *lepton* in ordinary matter. Electrons are found in the space around the nuclei of atoms.
electron-volt (eV)	the energy transferred when an *electron* (or another particle carrying the same size of charge as an electron) moves across a potential difference of 1 volt. $1\,\mathrm{MeV} = 10^6\,\mathrm{eV}$; $1\,\mathrm{GeV} = 10^9\,\mathrm{eV}$. $$1\,\mathrm{eV} = 1.602 \times 10^{-19}\,\mathrm{J} \approx 1.6 \times 10^{-19}\,\mathrm{J}$$
fission	when a large, unstable atomic nucleus splits into two smaller (but still quite large) nuclei. Fission only occurs at a significant rate if it induced by *neutrons*.
fundamental particles	particles of matter that cannot be split into smaller particles. Atoms were once thought to be fundamental, then protons neutrons and electrons and now quarks and leptons.
fusion	when two small atomic nuclei join together (fuse) to make a single, larger nucleus.
hadrons*	particles, made up from *quarks*, that are affected by the *strong force*. There are two groups of hadrons: *baryons* and *mesons*.
leptons*	are *fundamental particles* that are not affected by the *strong force*. *Electrons* are the leptons that we find in ordinary matter.
mesons*	are *hadrons* that consist of a *quark* and an anti-quark.
moderator	a substance that is used to reduce the kinetic energy of *neutrons*, via collisions, so that they more effectively induce nuclear *fission*.
neutrons*	electrically neutral *baryons* that are found in the nuclei of atoms. Free neutrons can induce nuclear *fission*, releasing further free neutrons.
nucleons	the particles – *neutrons* and *protons* – that are found in the nuclei of atoms. The <u>nucleon number</u> (A) of an atom is shown like this: ^{4}He.
nuclide	an atomic nucleus with a particular number of *protons* and *neutrons*. Isotopes of an element have the same number of protons but a different number of neutrons and so are different nuclides.
plasma	matter at a high temperature and consisting of charged particles (atomic nuclei and *electrons* that have been stripped from them).
protons*	positively charged *baryons* that are found in the nuclei of atoms. The <u>proton number</u> (Z) of an atom is shown like this: $_2$He.
quarks*	*fundamental particles* which make up *hadrons*. There are six types (or <u>flavours</u>) of quark: up, down, strange, charm, bottom and top (plus their anti-quarks).
radionuclides	unstable *nuclides* which decay, spontaneously and randomly, emitting radiation, to form more stable nuclides.
rest mass/energy	the mass/energy of a particle when it is stationary, i.e. has no kinetic energy. Mass and energy are related by the formula $E = mc^2$ so that the mass/energy of a particle can be given in *unified atomic mass units* or in *electron-volts*.
strong force	the force between nucleons that holds atomic nuclei together against the *Coulomb force* of repulsion between *protons*. The strong force acts between any pair of *hadrons*.
unified atomic mass units (u)	A unit of mass based on an atom of carbon-12 ($^{12}_{6}$C) having a mass of 12 u. [1 u = 931.5 MeV]
velocity of light (c)	An important factor in the mass/energy relationship $E = mc^2$ $c = 2.998 \times 10^8\,\mathrm{ms}^{-1} \approx 3 \times 10^8\,\mathrm{ms}^{-1}$
weak interaction	a force involved in *baryon* decay which can change the flavour of *quarks*. It is involved when a *radionuclide* decays with the emission of a beta (β) particle.

Index

Terms shown in **bold** also appear in the glossary (see page 91).
Pages in *italics* refer to figures.

α-particles, 10–11, 16, 20, 25, 33, 35, 74, 77
Anderson, Carl, 43, 44
anti-matter, 11, 42–3, 46, 61, 67–70, *71*, 73–4, 76, 77, 81
atomic number (Z), 2–4, 10, *10, 11*
atoms, 1–12, 40–1, *70*, 77–8, *79*

β-particles, 3, 11, 16–17, 20, 45, 74, 77–8
   see also electrons
barium-141, 16–17, 19
baryons, 66, 67–9, *67*, 72, 75–6, 81
Becquerel, Henri, 74
beryllium-9, 20
binding energy, 4, 5, 11–12, *12, 13*, 18, *18*, 28, *29*, 77
bubble chambers, 50, *50*, 60, 74

caesium-141, 3, 18, 19
carbon-12, 2, 32–3, *33*
carbon-14, 2, 3, 22–3
carbon cycle, 30, 32–3, *33*
chain reactions, 17, 20–1, 23
charm quark, 71, *71*
cloud chambers, 50, *50*
collisions, 47, 60–2, 69–70, 75
confinement, 35–7
control rods, 23–5, *24*
coolant, 24, *24*, 35
cosmic radiation, 43, 44, 54
Coulomb force (F), 5, 6, 8–10, 29–30, 32–4, 42
critical, 21, 23–5, *23, 24*
cyclotrons, 45, 56–8, *56*, 60, *60*

Dalton, John, 40, *41*
de Broglie, Louis, 43, 70
delayed neutrons, 20, 24
density (ρ), 7–8, 30, 32, 33, 37
deuterium, 4, 12, 22, *22*, 30–2, 34–7
Dirac, Paul, 43

Einstein, Albert, 11, 42–3, 47, 58, 70
electrical charge, 2–5, 29, 31, 44, 50, 51, 66, 67, 71, 73–4, 81
electricity generation, 24, *24*, 35, *36*
electromagnetic force, 42, 75, 76, 79
electromagnetic radiation, 29, 43, 59, 70, 74
electrons, 1, 3, 5, 34, 41–2, 43–4, 55–6, 70, 71, 73–4, 77
electron-volt (eV), 4, 48, 55
electrostatic (Coulomb) force, 5, 6, 8–10, 29–30, 32–4, 42
elements, 2, 40–1
energy distribution, 21–2, *21*
energy levels (shells), 2, 41
energy transfer, 4, 28–9, 33–5, 47, 70
environmental impacts, 26, 37
exchange particles, 79
excited state, 11

fast breeder reactors, 25–6
fast neutrons, 21, *23, 24*, 25
Fermi, Enrico, 45
fission, 3, 12, 16–27, *19*
fission bombs, 26
fission reactors, 21, 22–6, 35
fixed targets, 60, 61, 62
flavours, 67, 68, 70, 76, 77
Fleming's left-hand rule, 51, *51*

forces, 8, 41–2
Frisch, Otto, 16–17
fundamental particles, 40–6
fusion, 4–5, 12, 28–39
fusion reactors, 32, 33–4, *36*, 37, 74

γ-radiation, 11–12, 43–4, 74, 75
gas-cooled reactors, 24, *24*
Geiger, Hans, 41
Gell-Mann, Murray, 67, 71
gluons, 79
graphite blocks, 22–3, 25
gravitational force, 5, 6, 8, 32, 42, 75
gravitons, 79
ground state, 11

hadrons, 44, 45, 64–72
Hahn, Otto, 16, *17*, 20
half-lives, 11
heavy water, 22, *22*
helium-4, 2, 4, 5, *5*, 29, 31–3, 35, 37
high temperature, 29, 32–7
hydrogen atom, 5, *5*, 22, 29–33, 37
hydrogen cycle, 30–2

ignition, 35, 36, 37
inertial confinement, 37
intermediate vector bosons, 79
ionisation trails, 50, 51
iron-56, 12, 28, 33
isotopes, 2, 3

Joint European Torus (JET), 37
Joliot-Curie, Irene, 77

kinetic energy, 22–3, 29–30, 33, 35, 43, 47, 48, 51, 55–61, 69, 74
krypton-92, 17, 19

laser pulses, 37
Lawrence, Ernest, 56
leptons, 44, 71, 73–5, *75*, 77, 78, 81
liquid drop model, 18–19, *19*
lithium atoms, 2, 31, 41
lithium blanket, 35, *36*

magnetic confinement, 35–7, *35*
Marsden, Ernest, 41
mass, 7, 11–12, 18, 28–9, 32, 43, 47, 48, 58, 70, 77–8, *78*
mass number (A), 2–4, 6–7, *12*, 18, *19*, 28, 29, 78–9, *78*
Meitner, Lise, 16–17, *17*
Mendeleev, Dmitri, 40–1
mesons, 66, 68, 69, 71, 72, 76, 81
moderators, 22–3, *24*, 25
momentum, 60–1
muons, 44, 45, 73

natural fission, 20
neutrinos, 31, 32, 74–5, 77
neutron-induced fission, 3, 16–17, 19–24, *21, 24*
neutrons, 2, 3–6, 9–12, *10, 11*, 16–24, *21, 23, 24, 35, 36*, 41–2, 44, 76, 77–8, 81
nuclear energy, 17, 20–6
nuclear equations, 3–4
nuclear explosions, 25
nuclear fuel, 21–2, *24*, 25, 37
nuclear radius (r), 6–9, 7
nuclear reactions, 1, 3–5
nuclei, 1–15, 41, *70, 79*
nucleon (mass) number (A), 2–4, 6–7, *7, 12*, 18, *19*, 28, 29, 78–9, *78*

nucleons, 2, 5–12, *9, 13*, 18, *18*, 28, *29*, 42, *70, 79*
nuclides, 2, 3

particle accelerators, 44–5, 54–63, *54, 55*, 71
particle detection, 48–52
particle traces, 49–51, *49, 50*, 60
Pauli, Wolfgang, 74
periodic table, 40–1
phosphorus, 77
photoelectric effect, 43
photons, 43, 70, 79
pions, 44, 45, 47
Planck, Max, 70
plasma, 34, 35–7, *35*
plutonium-239, 21, 25–6
poloidal field, 36
positrons, 43–4, 50, *50*, 73, 77
potential energy, 11, 17–19, 29
Powell, Cecil, 44
pressurised water reactor, 24–5, *24*
proton (atomic) number (Z), 2–4, 10, *10, 11*
protons, 2, 4–7, 9–12, *9, 10*, 30–2, 41–2, 44, 47, 57–61, 71, 75, 76, 77–8, 81

quantum theory, 43, 70
quarks, 67–72, *68, 70, 71*, 75, *75*, 76, 77, 78, *79*, 81

Rabi, Isodor, 45
radioactive decay, 3, 10, 12, 74, 77
radionuclides, 3, 11, 77
relativity, 11, 43, 51, 58–9, 60, 61
reproduction factor, 23, 25
resonance frequency, 57
rest mass/energy, 11, 48–9, 71, 73, 74, 75, 76, 77, 81
rubidium-93, 3, 18, 19
Rutherford, Ernest, *41*

stability, 9–12, 18–20, 29–31
stars, 29–33, 34
steam generation, 24, *24*, 35, *36*
strangeness, 66, 67, 69, 76, 81
Strassman, Fritz, 16, 20
strong force, 6, 8–10, *9*, 29, 42, 44, 69, 73, 75, 76, 79
subcritical, 23–5
Sun, 29–33, 74–5
supercritical, 23, 25
supernova explosions, 33, *34*
synchrotrons, 59–60, *59, 60*, 61

thermal neutrons, 22, 23–4, *23, 24*
thermal reactors, 22–5, *23, 24*, 35
Thomson, J. J., 41
toroidal field, 36
transuranic elements, 16, 20
tritium, 22, 34–5, *36*, 37

unified atomic mass units (u), 4
Universe, 79, *79*
uranium-235, 3, 17–19, *19*, 20–3, 25
uranium-238, 16–17, 20, 21–2, 25
uranium-239, 21, 25

velocity of light (c), 4, 32, 48, 51, 58

water, 22, *22*
wavelength, 70
weak interaction, 75, 76–7, 79

Zweig, George, 67, 71